HELP!

My Financial Life SUCKS!

*A Step-by-Step Plan
for Financial Freedom!*

Michael J. White, CPA, CFP

OBP Inc.

The material contained in this book is general in nature and is not intended as specific advice on any particular matter. The author and publisher expressly disclaim any and all liability to any persons whatsoever in respect of anything done by any such person in reliance, whether in whole or in part, on this book. Any services, references, and/or websites that may be mentioned or referred to are provided for information purposes only. Please take appropriate legal or professional advice before acting on any information contained in this book.

CONTACT INFO
Michael J. White
Michael J. White CPA, CFP
5775 Los Angeles Ave., Suite 117
Simi Valley, CA 93063
Phone: 805.581.5400
Fax: 805.520.2809
www.michaeljwhite.com

CONTENTS

INTRODUCTION

America needs to go on a diet. A fiscal diet, that is, from national, state, and local government levels all the way down to each citizen. Over time, we have become programmed to spend, spend, and spend some more, whether we have the resources to spend or not.

In short, we spend more than we make.

In diet terms, losing weight is based on a simple equation: take in fewer calories than you burn. To achieve financial freedom, spend less than you make. We need to stop using credit cards irresponsibly, stop using our home as an ATM (although that has come to a grinding halt over the past few years), and stop giving in to all the advertising enticing us to purchase with zero down and payments beginning two years later.

What sounds too good to be true, really is too good to be true.

Let's spin it around. Would you like to obtain more wealth? The simple fact you are reading this book tells me you are committed to taking the necessary actions to achieve complete financial freedom. Committed, yes, but also unsure how to turn that commitment into action. Don't worry; if you bring the commitment, I'll provide the action plan. People who truly commit to building wealth become happier not because greater wealth automatically brings happiness, but because greater wealth can create greater opportunities. Wealth does not equal happiness, but wealth can provide greater freedom, freedom to choose. Think about it: When you are barely scraping by, living paycheck to paycheck, it doesn't feel as though you have many choices, does it? When you can choose, your life opens up in ways you haven't yet thought of.

Here's the best news of all: financial freedom can be yours no matter how much money you currently make. It's all about action.

Remember, what we think about, dream about, and wish for comes into our lives through action. T. Harv Ecker, author of *Secrets of the Millionaire Mind*, says, "What you focus on expands." That's why you should focus on wealth, not on debt. To obtain financial freedom, start by picturing a golden goose—your savings and investments—and then take action by feeding your golden goose every day.

I truly believe that if you see it, and believe it, you will achieve it. I've seen it happen for dozens of clients, and I've seen it happen in my life. When I was dating the girl who became my wife (we've been married for twenty-three years), she had a considerable amount of debt. I suggested minimizing the use of credit cards. I explained the importance of spending less than she made, of paying herself first, and of putting that money into savings. We talked a lot about living on a cash basis. If you find it hard to handle credit responsibly, living on a cash basis makes it easy because the most you can spend at any given moment is the money in your wallet or pocketbook.

She and I were just friends for about a year, until one day I realized I was spending a lot more time with her than with the girls I was dating. Because I am an accountant, I did a quick analysis: She was fun, beautiful, and smart. She loved kids and would be a great mother. She had all the qualities I looked for.

Although we had never talked about getting married, I knew she was the one. One night we were having dinner at one of our favorite restaurants, a quaint French restaurant called *Le Chene*. I had arranged with the chef to serve her favorite dessert, chocolate mousse, with the engagement ring displayed on top. I popped the question and she said yes. When it came to setting a date, I added one caveat: we would marry as soon as she paid off all her debts. Even though those debts seemed insurmountable—to her—we sat down and created a plan to pay off her debts in eighteen months. But eighteen months to her was too long. I have never seen anyone buckle down, get serious, and knock out a boatload of debt in such a short time.

If you want to get out of debt, you will find a way. I've seen it firsthand.

The key is to determine what you want. If you want to eliminate debt, build wealth and achieve financial freedom. I can help.

Let's get started.

CHAPTER ONE

Financial Freedom: The Basic Mindset

The term *life changing* gets thrown around much too easily. Seemingly, every diet, every exercise plan, even the average vacation package is advertised as life changing.

But here's the real deal: aside from improving your health or building better relationships with your loved ones, *nothing* you can do will change your life more dramatically than improving your financial health.

Think about it. If you're in debt (or worse, way over your head in debt), your everyday life is affected to an incredible degree. Bill collectors call; you agonize over every penny you spend; you hate facing your ever-growing stack of bills. There's no end and no relief in sight.

You probably try not to think about what life will be when you reach retirement age. You're much too busy worrying about today. When you do try to imagine a day when you can finally stop working , it's sad to imagine what life will be like when Social Security, and possibly a small pension, is all you'll have to live on.

Depressed yet? Don't be.

You've just started a journey that will change your life, starting today.

The solution starts with a problem. If you're like millions of people and you're struggling financially, there's a simple reason. It's not how much you earn or where you live or where you work. The problem is you're doing the same thing everyone around you is doing.

You're not alone. Estimates show 70 percent of Americans live paycheck to paycheck. Sadly, that creates an emotional toll: 37 percent of couples with marital problems report money as the main cause of their conflict.

Most people buy certain brands of clothes or makes of cars or even houses to fuel their self-esteem or to be someone they wish to be. Sure, designer labels can make you feel good. But does it really feel good living from paycheck to paycheck, wondering if you'll have enough money to pay the bills this month?

If you want to stand out from the crowd, be special, be unique, then get out of debt, make more money, and invest for a great retirement. Possibly retire early and you'll achieve something very few people accomplish. If you want your life to be different tomorrow, you have to make your life different today.

Be different today. As Dave Ramsey says, "If you will live like no one else, later you can *live* like no one else." Live simply. Buy used cars, used clothing, used exercise equipment, and used stuff you think you need. You end up paying 10 cents on the dollar and, as a result, can put money into your golden goose. By living simply today, you can be simply living when you retire.

To get you started, put a few steps in place.

Step 1: Commit

This is probably the most important step you can take. You must commit right now to start to change your financial life. You must commit to yourself to take the necessary steps to take control of your money and achieve the financial results you want.

Think about people you admire; I guarantee the first step they took on their path to success was to make a commitment to themselves that they would work hard and do whatever it took to reach their goal.

Step 2: Schedule Time to Focus on Your Finances

We all make time to eat, sleep, and go to work, but we rarely squeeze in a little time to focus on our money. Step 2 is to simply look at your daily schedule and make an appointment with yourself, every day, to spend time putting thought into action.

If you just try to get started "whenever," you'll find that weeks and months have flown by and you haven't taken action. If you really want to make changes in your finances that ultimately will affect your lifestyle and almost everything about your life, set aside time, every day, to take action. Sure, knowledge is power, but only action produces results.

If you're swamped with work, family, kids, and friends, schedule just thirty minutes a day. Don't have thirty minutes? Try turning off the TV instead of watching a half-hour show. Set your alarm to get up thirty minutes earlier, or stay up thirty minutes later at night. Create a list of everything you do in a day and see what lower priority activities you can cut back or cut out completely.

Remember, time management has nothing to do with managing *time*. Time management is about managing *ourselves*. If you're committed to becoming financially free, you can find at least thirty minutes a day.

Let's say you still can't find thirty minutes. (Hard for me to believe, but we'll pretend that it's true.) Try twenty. Or fifteen. Or ten. Any time spent working on your finances is better than none, which is what most people spend on theirs. Of course, the more time you spend, the better.

The key is consistency. Spend time *every day* working on your finances. Make taking control of your money a habit. Habits, both good and bad, are built over time. The longer you do something, the more likely you are to continue to do that something. So build the good habit of spending a little time every day focused on your finances. Soon it will be second nature, and you won't give it a thought.

Here are some tricks to help you lock in your daily habit:

- Find a twelve-month calendar with a box for every day. A wall calendar is probably best, but any calendar, as long as it has a box for each day, is OK.
- Every day you work on your finances, whether you're evaluating your finances or learning more about money and investing, use a Magic Marker and put a big "*X*" inside the box for that day. Make sure to keep your calendar where it's easily visible so you can see whether you've crossed off today's box.
- After a few days of taking action and crossing off boxes, you'll start to build a chain of *X*s. A chain of *X*s show you're taking positive actions. Then make it your goal never to break the chain. That's right. From the moment you start, your goal, for the rest of your life, is, as it says in the Fleetwood Mac song, to "never break the chain."

Simple method, sure, but does it work?

It worked for Jerry Seinfeld. Every day Seinfeld spent time writing new jokes and, and he put a big red *X* on his calendar when he was done. Whether he was traveling on an airplane, busy with meetings, or busy with family, he spent time writing new material every day and marked off another day on the calendar. By making a commitment to himself to "never break the chain," Seinfeld became a famous comedian and a rich one too.

If it worked for Jerry Seinfeld, it can work for you too.

Bottom line. The more time you spend changing your financial life, the more money you put in your pocket. Doesn't that make scheduling time worth it?

Step 3: Start Where You Are *Today*

Everyone's personal situation is different. Some people are deep in debt. Others have little or no debt and are interested only in making more money and retiring sooner. Some already have high incomes, whereas others may be living paycheck to paycheck as they struggle to get by.

It's important for you to start where you are today. Fully understanding your situation helps you make smart decisions about changing your situation.

Remember, no matter where you are today, you can get to a better place tomorrow.

Step 4: Act

Achieving financial freedom is built on a number of action steps. Again, knowledge is important, but action is the key to becoming financially free. After all, you can *know* what to do, but if you don't *do* it, you will never get the results you want.

As you work your way through this book, follow the steps and put them into action. Some steps may feel new and uncomfortable, but that's OK. Trying new things and building new habits almost always feels a little awkward at first.

Think of it this way: riding a bike doesn't come naturally to most kids, but after a lot of trial and error (and maybe even some skinned knees and bruises), most kids figure it out and become expert bike riders.

You can become an expert at taking control of your finances if you push past any uncomfortable or awkward feelings and continue to act daily, consistently.

It's like learning to ride a bike. If you fall down, it's important that you get up, dust yourself off, and try again. You fail only if you stop trying.

Before you start trying, the key is to change how you think about money and finances. Otherwise, you'll continue to make the same financial mistakes based on incorrect information and erroneous beliefs.

So let's take a few minutes to change how you look at money.

Change Your Financial Mindset

First, let's debunk a few myths and along the way uncover some important facts about money, spending, and personal finance.

- **You are not alone.** Most people have money problems. Some are just good at hiding the fact. For example, recent studies show that two out of ten people are at serious risk of foreclosure, and one of five is currently behind on mortgage payments. Let's put that in real terms. Next time you're in a restaurant, look around. If there are forty people seated around you, eight of them are trying to figure out how to save their homes, and ten or more are behind and are trying to figure out how they'll come up with the money to pay their bills next month. (A thought that might make you wonder why they are in the restaurant at all if they are having money problems.)

- **You are not a bad person if you don't have complete control over your finances.** Most of us know math and English and history. We learned those subjects in school. Most schools don't teach personal finance. What most of us know we learned through trial and a lot of error. If you're struggling, you shouldn't be ashamed or embarrassed. Use those feelings to get motivated to change.

- **You can change your financial life.** Others have, even people who were in worse shape than you are. For example, *Forbes* magazine estimates that almost two-thirds of the world's billionaires built their fortunes from scratch, relying on determination and hard work. Think of it this way: your success is limited only by your imagination and by how hard you're willing to work at changing your life. Although not everyone becomes a multimillionaire, with time and effort anyone can become debt free and build a retirement nest egg.

- **Financial freedom is 80 percent behavior management and 20 percent math.** Any successful financial system requires managing yourself, not your money. That's why, for individuals, *money management* is the wrong term. If you manage *yourself,* your money takes care of itself. You don't need to be a math expert or a financial wizard; you just have to learn to make smart decisions.

- **Financial freedom does not require "living poor."** Instead, taking control of your finances allows you to live a better quality of life. Rich people are unhappy too. Money doesn't cure problems; in some instances, it magnifies personal problems. You can live within your means and have a great life. Your day-to-day quality of living can actually increase as you start saving more money and paying down debt.

- **Advertisers want you to spend, and they don't care about your debt.** We live in a consumer-based society and are bombarded with advertisements that create false beliefs. Ads tell that ownership of stuff increases your self-worth; shopping can help you decrease stress; things can make you feel good. Think about the stereotypical midlife crisis where a fifty-year-old man buys a $100,000 sports car. Maybe the car makes him feel better; maybe it doesn't. All we know for certain is that his bank balance was significantly reduced by the purchase.

- **Taking control takes time, but so does achieving anything worthwhile.** You won't become debt free and rich overnight. It takes time, but if you do just a little bit every day, you'll see amazing results. The longer you wait to start, the longer it will take.

Making lots of money is a great thing. We all have the capacity to make lots of money, even though most people limit their ability. Sometimes we have to stop and erase our hard drive and reprogram it with the right attitude and files to start making lots of money.

I know. I had to.

My Story

I made a lot of money early in my life only to lose most of it in the stock market in the late 1990s and early 2000s. I lost most of it during the tech-bubble crash.

Leverage almost killed me. In the stock market, the use of leverage is quite common. For example, if you have $5,000 to invest, you can, under certain conditions, use that $5,000 to control $10,000 or $20,000 or more worth of stock. The difference in what you pay and what you control is called *margin*. Using margin is a two-edged sword, great when prices are going higher but devastating when stock prices fall. When prices fall too far, you get a margin call from your broker asking you to deposit more money in your account to cover your losses, even if those losses are only on paper at that point.

Here's what happened to me. I bought stock on margin, and when the market dipped, I ignored all my rules of investing and let emotions take over my decision-making process. I did not use stop–losses and started getting margin calls asking me for more money. I didn't have more money, so they sold the shares I owned to cover my losses. I ignored the problem and put my head in the sand, and one day I had nothing left. I had the wrong frame of mind, and it almost destroyed me and my family.

Mostly, I made a lot of excuses. As Richard Carlson says in his book *Don't Worry, Make Money*, "You can make excuses, and you can make money, but you can't do both." Excuses are nothing more than an expression of fear. Successful people face the same fears and frustrations as everyone else. The difference is successful people don't hesitate; they take action. Action is the key. Rather than becoming overwhelmed by **negative** thoughts, take action and you can overcome fear.

Do what *needs* to be done today so you can do what you *want* to do tomorrow.

Now that you have begun to change your mindset and determine your individual motivations and incentives for taking control and achieving financial freedom, let's put some concrete behaviors in place to help reinforce your new mindset. We'll start by focusing on what you make and, more important, what you spend.

Take-Away Points

1. Nothing you can do will change your life more dramatically than improving your financial health.
2. If you want your life to be different tomorrow, you have to make your life different today.
3. You must commit to take the necessary steps to take control of your finances.
4. Action is the key to becoming financially free.
5. Financial freedom is 80% behavior management, 20% math.
6. If you manage yourself, your money will take care of itself.
7. Do what needs to be done today so you can do what you want to do tomorrow.
8. Simply your lifestyle, to multiply your wealth.

CHAPTER TWO

Determining Where You Are

L et's start with a basic premise. Before you start thinking about paying off your debts, you first need to stop spending yourself into a hole. Remember, if you're in a hole, the easiest way to get out of the hole is to first stop digging.

We said we would start with where you are today. So here is what we will do:

- Determine your true net income
- Determine your current net worth
- Determine exactly how you spend your money

Then, in the next chapter, we will

- Decrease your spending immediately
- Build a monthly budget
- Create a system to help you stay on track

The action steps in these two chapters create the foundation for success in future chapters. So don't skip ahead, and don't be tempted to take shortcuts. This phase of achieving financial freedom certainly isn't easy, and it may force you to confront a few of your personal financial demons. But by the end you'll realize it was fun and definitely worth it, financially and, just as important, emotionally.

Step 1: Determine Your True Net Income

Let's do a little exercise. Don't skip this. It's incredibly important, and it will change how you think about money—*your* money—forever.

We'll start with a simple premise. You know what you make.

Well, at least you know your hourly rate or your weekly or monthly salary. When you fill out your taxes, you know your gross income for the year. And when you receive your paycheck, you definitely know how much cash you get to spend.

The cash you get on payday is your net income—that's the number that matters the most, at least for our purposes.

You probably don't give your income a second thought, other than probably to wish you made more. That's a major problem. If you truly understand what you *earn*, you can better evaluate what you *spend*, and you can make better decisions about where and how you spend your hard-earned money. If you don't clearly understand what your true income is, you can easily fall into the mistake of spending more money on some items than you really want to, or ever should.

So let's dig deeper into your income. Follow along on this worksheet; fill in your actual pay in place of the sample figures I've provided. This math exercise will definitely change your behaviors.

Say a fictitious person (we'll call her Mary) makes $50,000 per year. In 2009 the total per capita personal income—per capita means per *person*, not per *family*—in the United States was just over $39,000. If she earns $50,000, she's making well above the average.

Yearly Income	Mary $50,000	Your Income _____

Now divide $50,000 by 2,080 to determine Mary's hourly rate. If you are paid by the hour, you already know your hourly rate, so you can skip this step. The number of hours you work in a year is 2,080 if you work forty-hour weeks (40 × 52 = 2,080).

Hourly Rate	**Mary**	**Your Hourly Rate**
	$50,000 / 2080 = $24.04	_____

So, Mary's hourly rate is $24.04; we'll round it off to $24 to make the math easier from this point on. That means every hour she works, she earns $24, right? Oops. Not so fast.

Let's look at her deductions. Say she is enrolled in a 401(k) plan and contributes 5 percent of her gross income each pay period. Enrolling in a 401(k) plan is an excellent idea, by the way. These plans are arguably the best investment available for the average American.

Now, 5 percent of $24/hour is $1.20, so she now has $22.80 left in net income. That's OK. The 401(k) is a great investment in her future and well worth the "loss" of income.

Let's keep going. We'll assume Mary is paid every week, so she makes $961.54 per week gross. You can fill in this chart using your weekly, biweekly, or monthly pay stub, depending on how you're paid. Here are some common income deductions. Check out your pay stub to see exactly what your deductions are.

	Mary	**Yours**
Gross Income	$961.54	_____
401(k) deduction	$48.08	_____
Federal taxes	$137.02	_____
State taxes	$50.34	_____
Social Security	$56.63	_____
Health insurance	$85	_____
Miscellaneous	$0	_____
Net Income	$580.01	_____

Use your pay stub to fill in your own deductions and calculate your own net income. Then divide your net income by the hours in that pay period. So, if you are paid

Weekly	Divide your pay by 40
Biweekly (every two weeks)	Divide your pay by 80
Bimonthly (twice a month)	Divide by 86.67
	(2,080 / 24 pay periods)
Monthly	Divide by 17.33

For example:

Mary's Weekly Income	**Divided by**	**Equals Her Hourly Rate**
$580.01	/40	= $14.50

Your Net Income	**Divided by**	**Equals Your Hourly Rate**
_____	/_____	= $_____

After all your deductions, determine your net—again, the amount of money you bring home—hourly income. If we assume Mary has no other miscellaneous deductions, using the example just mentioned, her $24 per hour is, in reality, $14.50 in actual, spendable dollars.

That means her take-home pay is only 60 percent of her gross income, which, by the way, is about what the average American in her situation brings home.

You probably realize by now that you could simply divide your net pay by your hours per pay period to get the same answer. The reason we worked our way through the complete example is so you have a good feel for where a major chunk of your hard-earned money goes. Although you can't control taxes (not completely, anyway), you *can* control other financial decisions and outcomes.

It's important that you know your net income. The goal is for you to understand your true income so you can make decisions based on that number. Here's a simple example:

- In her mind, Mary makes $24 an hour. Substitute your own amount.
- She hires a lawn service to cut her grass. They charge her $25 per cutting. (In most areas $25 is probably a low figure for a professional lawn care service.)
- She could do it herself—after all, it takes only forty-five minutes—but it's a hassle, and, after all, she's *way* too busy. And she makes $24 an hour, so paying someone else to take care of cutting the grass sounds pretty good, all things considered.
- But then she evaluates the cost of having someone else cut her grass using her true hourly income. In reality she brings home only $14.50. That's the cash she gets, in her pocketbook, for an hour's work. She'll have to work 1.7 hours to make the $25 to pay the lawn service.

Mary now needs to decide if she should put in 1.7 hours of work at her job or forty-five minutes of work at home. Using her true income, she needs to decide what makes more sense for her now.

Or look at it another way. Imagine you work eight hours a day at Mary's net hourly rate, and you bring home $116 per day. Not bad, but do you really want to spend every day, $4.50 on a cappuccino, $12 eating lunch out, $5 on cigarettes, and maybe even a couple of dollars on lottery tickets? Should 15 percent to 20 percent of your take-home pay be spent on those items?

If you look at how you spend your money from that perspective, those spending choices seem unwise.

Your time has value. Your work time has value in terms of what you're paid, and your free time away from work has personal value. Understanding what you truly make per hour while you are working can help you better evaluate what you are willing to do— and willing to spend. Don't overestimate your true hourly income.

Your real, spendable hourly income is all that matters when you evaluate an expense or a purchase.

Before we move on, take a second to determine your actual monthly income on a weekly and monthly basis. You'll use those figures later. Simply multiply your hourly income by 40 to get your weekly income.

For example, if you bring home $14.50 an hour, as Mary does, your weekly spendable income is $580. Multiply your weekly income by 4.25—that's how many weeks are in the average month—to calculate your monthly income (52 / 12 = 4.25). In this example, although your gross is $4,086 per month, your take-home pay is $2,465 per month. That's what you get to spend.

Depressed? Don't be. Things will get better. I Promise.

Now let's look at your net worth.

Step 2: Determine Your Net Worth

Your net worth, in simple terms, is the difference in what you own and what you owe (assets – liabilities = net worth).

Let's start with your assets. Assets are cash or items that can be turned into cash.

Bank accounts, stock investments, and the like are assets.

Your home is an asset, as long as it has equity, meaning it is worth more, in terms of real market value, than what you owe. If you could sell your house for $300,000 and you owe only $250,000, you have $50,000 in equity. That equity is an asset.

If your car is paid off and you could sell it for $5,000, it's an asset. If you just bought a car and you put little or no money down, even though it's worth $20,000, it's not an asset because if you sold it today, the proceeds wouldn't go into your pocket; they would go to paying off your car loan.

Sound complicated? Don't worry. I'll help you figure it all out.

Use the following worksheet to list all your assets. Remember, actual value is what you can sell the item for, not what it is theoretically worth. A diamond necklace that *costs* $800 isn't *worth* $800 unless someone will actually pay you that much for it.

To get you thinking, here's a list of some common assets you might have:

- Savings accounts, checking accounts, investment accounts
- 401(k) accounts, retirement accounts, life insurance policies (cash value, not the policy value)
- Home
- Automobiles, motorcycles, boats, RVs
- Jewelry
- Furniture
- Collectibles
- Antiques
- Artwork
- Cash

Now fill out your sheet:

Your Assets

Cash	_____
Checking account	_____
Savings account	_____
Money market funds	_____
Home(s)	_____
Life insurance (cash value)	_____
Stocks	_____
Mutual funds	_____
IRA	_____
401(k)	_____
Retirement plan (current value)	_____
Automobile(s)	_____
Jewelry	_____
Antiques and collectibles	_____
Furniture	_____
Other	_____
Total Assets	$_____

List everything, but don't be tempted to overestimate values. It's easy to place emotional value on an item that has no bearing on its actual value. Your father's watch may be priceless—to you—but worth only $20 to a person who had no relationship with your father. Here's an easy way to approach valuing your assets: consider what all your possessions would be worth if you died and they had to be sold.

Now that you've listed your assets, it's time to list your liabilities. Liabilities are what you owe. Any debt is a liability: credit cards, personal loans, mortgages, car loans, even money you owe to friends or family.

Determining your liabilities is easier than determining your assets. In most cases you get a bill or a statement, unless a friend loaned you some money. Regardless, that's still a liability. Most people have liabilities like these:

- Credit cards
- Car loans
- Mortgage
- Medical bills
- Child support and alimony
- Other debts
- Personal loans

Use the following worksheet to list your liabilities. Again, list everything. Take the time to think it through. It may be a painful and depressing exercise, but don't be tempted to hide from reality. Remember, you're starting from where you are today. You must know your current situation so you can make good decisions and take steps to improve it.

Now fill out your sheet:

Your Liabilities

Mortgage	_____
Credit cards	_____
	_____
	_____
Automobile loans	_____
	_____
Medical bills	_____
Personal loans	_____
Student loans	_____
Store loans	_____
	_____
Alimony and child support	_____
Other	_____
	_____
Total Liabilities	$_____

Now that you've determined what you have (your assets) and what you owe (your liabilities), simply subtract your liabilities from your assets to determine your net worth.

[total assets (_____) – total liabilities (_____) = net worth]

For example, if you have $500,000 in assets and $480,000 in liabilities, your net worth is $20,000. The greater your net worth, the better off you are. But even if you have a negative net worth, meaning you owe more than you own, don't worry. You will take steps that will put you on the right path.

Determining your net worth may not be a fun exercise, but it's an incredibly valuable exercise that helps change your mindset and sets the stage for achieving financial freedom.

Quick note. It's easy to fool yourself into thinking you have a high net worth because you have equity in your home. Say your home has a fair market value of $400,000 and you owe $350,000. The result is an asset worth $50,000. But wait. We all have to live somewhere, and can you quickly access that money in an emergency? Maybe, maybe not. Just don't be tempted to think you're in great shape because you have money in your home. Even if you sell the home to tap the equity, you still need a place to live and you still have to spend money for housing.

Step 3: Determine Your Actual Spending

No matter how much money we have, all of us, at least at times, spend without thought. We have all gone to the store and bought things we didn't plan to purchase—or even need—simply because they were on sale. Maybe you bought another bottle of shampoo when you already have six or eight hiding in various bathroom closets and cabinets. Or maybe, on the other end of the spending spectrum, you bought a new car when the old car was just fine, and maybe even already paid off.

Now say you've decided to purchase something you only "want" but don't need, for example, a new car. If you don't need a new car, the only potential benefit to the purchase is a tax reduction, provided it is used for business purposes. If the car costs $30,000, you may save $10,000 in taxes, but you are out of pocket $20,000. If you instead invest that $20,000 in a mutual fund, average an annual return of 8 percent over thirty years, and add no additional funds to the account, your original $20,000 turns into approximately $239,000.

The difference lies in what economists refer to as *opportunity cost*. Opportunity cost, simply put, is what else you could do with money instead of buying "stuff". If you buy a new car instead of a used car, the difference in price is the opportunity cost. Think what else you could have done with that money. Everything you buy loses value as soon as you purchase it. I've known a number of people at retirement age who have very little in savings, but they drove nice cars for years. In the process, they lost hundreds of thousands of dollars in opportunity cost. I know: sometimes it feels great to buy a new car. But nothing feels better than buying the car of your dreams with cash, secure in the knowledge you have the financial ability to do so.

To get control of your finances, you have to figure out what you *really* spend, not just what you *think* you spend.

By the way, this step is most people's least favorite thing to do, which is why most people live beyond their means and make poor financial decisions. No pain, no gain definitely applies here.

On the other hand, if at the end of the month you've thought, "Wait a minute; where did all my money go?" Well, now you'll know.

To determine what you actually spend, first, gather up all your bills. Your bills show your actual expenses for loans, utility payments, everything. Your credit card statements also show you how much you spend on certain items. Pull out as many old credit card statements as you can. They'll help you identify spending you may not remember. Then list all the ways you spend money, especially cash, that don't show up on a monthly bill.

And while you're at it, think about where you were when you spent your money. Look at the charges on your credit card bills and think about where you were—mentally and, just as important, physically—when you made those purchases. What mood were you in? Did you spend the day at the mall because you were bored? Did you flip channels aimlessly and on the spur of the moment decide to buy something you never use? If you did need an item, could you have done a little comparison shopping and found a better value? Instead of buying the amount or size you purchased should you have bought less? (Will you really ever use the twelve–pack of tomato sauce you bought at the bulk-purchase store?)

Use this worksheet to help you determine your monthly expenses. The list isn't exhaustive. You are likely to have expenses not listed here, so write them in. Just make sure you list *everything*.

Quick note. No matter how hard you try, you may not remember all your weekly or monthly expenses. Take a month and track every penny you spend. Every time you write a check, use your credit card, or pay cash, write it down. You'll be surprised by how many ways you spend money that have become so automatic you don't even think about them much less remember them.

Expenses

Rent/mortgage	_____
Car payment	_____
Car payment	_____
Credit card payment	_____
Credit card payment	_____
Credit card payment	_____
Car insurance	_____
Gas and car repairs	_____
Home insurance	_____
Other loans	_____
Life insurance	_____
Childcare and tuition	_____
Groceries	_____
Utility bills	_____
Phone bills	_____
Internet	_____
Cable bill	_____
Clothing	_____
Meals (out)	_____
Entertainment	_____
Other	_____
Other	_____
Total Expenses	$_____

I know: it can be mentally exhausting to put together your list of expenses, especially if you've put your financial life on autopilot for a long time. But remember, knowledge is power, and if you have quit thinking about how you spend your money, you have no power. You may also get angry. I know people who wanted to throw up when they realized they were still making payments on things they hadn't used or enjoyed or couldn't even *find* in months.

For example, are you paying off a home equity loan that you used to pay off credit cards? I hope you aren't, but if you are like many Americans, you very well could be. Using a home equity loan may be a good idea to eliminate higher interest rates, but not if you turn around and use those credit cards again. In addition, you are probably spreading those payments over fifteen, twenty, or even thirty years, so you could end up paying more in total interest than you would have on the credit card.

We'll look at ways to reduce your expenses later; for now, simply identify everything you spend money on. *Everything.*

Before you move on, double-check to make sure you didn't miss anything. Have your spouse look it over too. Find everything you spend money on. You need to know where you are today.

Notice how your expenses fall into two broad categories: fixed expenses and variable expenses. Fixed expenses are things you spend money on that you can't easily control or change. For instance, your rent or mortgage payment is a fixed expense. You can't quickly reduce or eliminate that spending. Insurance is also a fixed expense. Although you could shop for a cheaper rate, relatively speaking, you can't decide today that you'll pay less for car insurance. Even so, we will look at reducing that a little later.

But you can decide to start bringing your lunch to work today, which immediately reduces your spending. Groceries, entertainment, gas, clothing—all those are variable expenses because you can easily make different decisions that can reduce your spending.

Take a second and look at your expenses worksheet, noting which items are variable expenses and which are truly fixed expenses. For example, you may have entered $65 for your cable bill. You probably see that as a fixed expense because it's a bill you pay every month. But in reality cable is a variable expense. You could drop cable service altogether, or more realistically you could stop paying for premium channels you really don't watch. That's why cable is a variable expense. You can immediately decide to spend less. Almost every expense category on your sheet can, with a little creativity and a willingness to change your outlook on spending, be reduced, which puts more money in your pocket.

Before we move on, let's perform a quick sense–check of your current financial position. Subtract all your current monthly expenses, fixed and variable, from the monthly net income you've calculated.

We didn't fill out an expense worksheet for Mary, so for the sake of this example, let's pretend she spends $2,258 per month. Here's where she stands on a monthly basis:

[net income ($2,465) – expenses ($2,258) = surplus ($207)]

Mary has $207 left over each month after all her bills and expenses are paid.

Now write in your numbers:

[net income (_____) – expenses (_____) = your monthly surplus/shortfall (_____)]

If you spend less than you earn, that's great, but you can do better. If you spend more than you earn, you're in trouble, but you can turn that situation around. If you're like most people, you fall into one of three categories:

1. Expenses are less than your income, and you are able to put money away each month.
2. Typical monthly expense are reasonable or within your income, but the extras get you in trouble.
3. Typical monthly expenses, not even counting the extras, are too much for your income level.

Again, no matter where you currently fall, you can do better. What's important is that now, possibly for the first time, you understand exactly where you stand today.

Now let's make where you stand a lot better.

Take-Away Points

1. **The easiet way to get out of a hole is to first stop digging.**
2. **Know your true income so you can make informed decisions.**
3. **You must know your current situation to set the stage to make the right decisions to achieve financial freedom.**
4. **Opportunity cost is what else you could do with the money instead of buying "stuff".**
5. **Track every nickle you spend for two months. By knowing where all your money goes, you can make better decisions.**
6. **Knowledge is power.**

CHAPTER THREE

Keeping More by Managing Debt

Now for the fun part.

Step 4: Decrease Your Spending

Once you know how you spend your money, reducing your expenses is a lot easier than you might have imagined. The process of determining your net worth and listing your possessions should have made you question a lot of the spending choices you've made in the past. That's one of the biggest reasons you went through those steps. Now you understand not only the nuts and bolts of your personal financial decisions but also your emotional reaction to your money and how you spend it.

It's not how much you make if you spend it all. In the end what matters is how much you have left. Even if you don't make a lot of money, you can live well if you don't waste what you earn.

Quick note. This is a large section. But don't worry if it seems overwhelming at first. At the end is a worksheet to help you, step by step, put this process into practice.

Go back to your expenses worksheet. Look at each category. Pull out the bills or statements that document your spending in that category. Then ask yourself the following questions for each item in that category:

- **Can I get rid of this expense completely?** For example, you may pay a monthly fee for cell phone insurance. Typically, that insurance costs around $5 per month. Does it make sense to have insurance if it costs only $90 to replace the cell phone and the deductible is $50? Cutting off the insurance pays for itself in eight months. A fee of $5 per month may not sound like much, but it adds up to $60 per year you are in effect giving away.

- **If I can't get rid of the expense, can I at least reduce the amount?** To use the cell phone example again, say you pay $10 per month to send 200 text messages and an additional $10 because you always go over your limit. Can you convert to an unlimited plan for $12 per month? Or can you decide the opportunity to text isn't really that important and eliminate the charge altogether? Examine every bill, and consider calling to ask for a rate reduction. If you're not sure, just make the call and ask. All they can say is no.

- **If I can't reduce the amount, is there another option to save money?** Let's use cell phones again. Your cell phone plan costs $50, and you get unlimited minutes, including long distance. You also have phone service in your house that costs $45 per month. Do you need both phone services? Can you eliminate your home phone service and simply use your cell phone for all calls? Lots of people do.

If you are willing to be creative and make a few changes, you can find lots of ways to save. For example:

- **Phone, cable, and Internet service.** Many cable companies and phone companies offer complete packages that provide bundles of services. If you get cable Internet, you may be able to add digital phone service. And if you add in cable, and drop some of your premium channels, you might be able to add services and still pay less. Cable providers and phone providers love bundles. Take advantage.

- **Credit cards.** If you want to pay less in interest, call your credit card company and ask for a lower interest rate. Just tell them you want to have your interest rate reduced or you will switch to another credit card. Sometimes your first attempt will fail; if that happens, ask for a supervisor. It's worth it. If you have a $10,000 balance on your card and your rate is reduced by as little as 2 percent, you'll save $200 a year in interest. Say it takes you a couple of hours to work your way through the system and get a reduction. In the end you will have made $100 an hour for making phone calls. Not bad.

- **Car insurance.** Scrutinize your policy on every year. If you didn't get a ticket or have an accident last year, call and ask for a rate reduction. You never get what you don't ask for. So ask.

- **Meals.** For most people, eating out is a habit, not a necessity. That's especially true where lunches are concerned. Start bringing your lunch to work. You instantly save money, especially if you bring leftovers. If you like to get out of the office or workplace during lunch, take a walk, eat outside, or eat in the cafeteria. Say you spend $6 on every lunch every workday. Over the course of a year, you'll spend about $1,500 just for the privilege of going out to lunch. If your net income is, like Mary's, $14.50 per hour, you'll work more than two weeks paying for your lunches over the course of a year. When viewed from that perspective, does it still seem worth it?

I've just listed a few possibilities. I feel sure you have already thought of other ways you can save money.

But before we move on to the next step and change your spending mindset, make sure you pay close attention to the nitty-gritty of your spending. When you get a bill or an invoice, look at the fine print every time. If you are like most people, bills become automatic. You look at the amount you have to pay and ignore the rest. The devil is in the details. Your financial future might be hiding in the details. For example, take a close look at your credit card statements. It's possible that

- You signed up for a credit monitoring service that charges a fee every month
- You still pay for landline phone service even though you thought you disconnected it
- You pay an annual fee for an online service, for a website, or for a subscription you no longer use or even remember you have

Check your credit card bill each month. Don't just look for errors or mistakes; look for services or items you are paying for that you no longer use or maybe even have forgotten. If a little detective work fails to turn up a mistake or an expense you forgot, I will be surprised.

Change Your Spending Mindset

Now let's take the process a step further. Studies show when people use plastic they spend 17 percent to 21 percent more on discretionary items than when they use cash. In a household making $100,000 a year, that family spends $17,000 to $21,000 more on "stuff" than if they had used cash. That's money they could have been used to pay down debt or to save for retirement. Plastic is convenient but a convenience that can destroy your finances.

By the same token, comparison shopping, looking for discounts, and even eliminating some spending is important. But at the core of a lasting behavior change is developing the ability, and habit, of making better overall buying decisions. Remember, we live in a consumer society that programs us all to buy, buy, buy. However, you can exercise control and make your own decisions. Here are some ways to help ensure you make great spending decisions:

- **Walk away.** It's easy to make a spur-of-the-moment purchase. The problem is you're likely to feel some degree of buyer's remorse if you purchase based on emotions or a whim. Take the emotion out of your decision by waiting for a day. If you still feel the same way about the purchase the next day, go for it. In a lot of cases, you will find that walking away gives you a very different perspective on the purchase.

- **Decide exactly why you want to buy.** Nothing you buy makes you feel better about yourself, unless you make a wise, well-reasoned purchase. Buying things to impress your buddies does not make you feel better over the long term. Happiness is never for sale, so think about why you want to buy a particular item. And if you are not sure of your reasons, or cannot clearly explain those reasons to yourself or to someone else in rational terms, then walk away.

- **Think about other uses of that money.** Spending $60,000 (or more because of the interest you will pay if you don't pay cash) for a new car means $60,000 will not go into an investment account. Sure, you own the car, but the money you spent is gone forever. Weigh the alternative of every expense, especially when you consider making a major expense. Just think what you could do with the $10,000 or $20,000 you save by buying a less-expensive car.

Studies show people exhibit psychological and physical reactions when they spend large amounts of money. One study showed that people's heart rates increase, people start to sweat, and people feel anxious when they spent more than $300. It's a natural response, so take advantage of the anxiety you feel. If you are nervous about a purchase, that's a sign that you're not ready. Listen to your body. Walk away, sleep on it, make sure you understand what you are giving up by making a purchase, and you'll make better spending decisions.

Still not convinced you can do it? Let's do an exercise:

Reduce Your Spending

Right now you're probably thinking, "Wow! That's a lot to do. I understand it all, but where do I start?"

Let's make it easy. Following is a worksheet to help you work through almost all your expenses and find ways to reduce spending, in many cases painlessly. Simply fill out the worksheet and then every day use the time you have scheduled to work on your finances to take care of the next items on the list.

Here's an example. The following are some of Mary's monthly expenses. We'll use a part of the worksheet to help you understand what to do.

Expense	Current Amount	Action Taken	New Amount
Cell phone	$65		
Car insurance	$50		
Lunch (work)	$160		

So far, we've simply listed the current amount Mary spends on a few items. Later you will list everything you spend because each item is a potential source of savings.

Now we'll do a little work:

Expense	Current Amount	Action Taken	New Amount
Cell phone	$65	Changed plan	$45
Car insurance	$50	Dropped towing	$45
Lunch (work)	$160	Bring from home	$80

After listing her expenses, Mary called her cell phone provider and dropped replacement insurance and switched to unlimited texting between other people using the same carrier. Everyone in her family uses the same carrier, and she decides that works for her. She also dropped towing insurance for her car since because in eight years she's never needed it. She also learned her teenage son could qualify for a lower rate if he makes the honor roll, so she'll keep that in mind for later. And, she started taking her lunch to work (she was throwing away leftovers anyway). But she figures she may have to buy a little more food at the grocery store, so she estimates she can reduce that expense at least by half.

For doing about twenty minutes of work, she saved $20 on her cell phone bill, $5 on her car insurance bill, and $80 on lunch. That's $105 per month, which, if you remember, takes her 6.7 hours to earn, based on her true income. In effect she's *made* $105 dollars each month for twenty minutes of work.

Here's what you do. First, fill in the first two columns of this reduce spending worksheet. Then, every day work on reducing the expense in one, two, five, however many entries on the list you have time for. Write down your savings. That will make you feel good about your efforts. And if you start to lose motivation, remember that if you can save $20 per month after putting in an hour's time on the phone, for example, that's like making $240 an hour because you'll save $240 per year for that one hour's work.

Let's get started on your worksheet. On the following worksheet are common categories; at the bottom are a number of blank lines you can use to fill in your unique expense items and categories.

Reduce Spending

Expense	Current Amount	Action Taken	New Amount
Rent/mortgage	_____	_____	_____
Car payment	_____	_____	_____
Car payment	_____	_____	_____
Credit card	_____	_____	_____
Credit card	_____	_____	_____
Credit card	_____	_____	_____
Car insurance	_____	_____	_____
Gas	_____	_____	_____
Parking/tolls	_____	_____	_____
Home insurance	_____	_____	_____
Other loans	_____	_____	_____
Other loans	_____	_____	_____
Life insurance	_____	_____	_____
Child care	_____	_____	_____
Groceries	_____	_____	_____
Utilities	_____	_____	_____
Utilities	_____	_____	_____
Utilities	_____	_____	_____
Phone	_____	_____	_____
Internet	_____	_____	_____
Cable	_____	_____	_____
Clothing	_____	_____	_____
Meals (out)	_____	_____	_____
Entertainment	_____	_____	_____
_____	_____	_____	_____
_____	_____	_____	_____
_____	_____	_____	_____
_____	_____	_____	_____
_____	_____	_____	_____
_____	_____	_____	_____
_____	_____	_____	_____

_____	_____	_____	_____
_____	_____	_____	_____
_____	_____	_____	_____
_____	_____	_____	_____
_____	_____	_____	_____
_____	_____	_____	_____
_____	_____	_____	_____

If you're not sure how to reduce an expense, it's easy. *Ask.* Most companies don't want to lose your business. As I mentioned before, say you want to reduce the interest rate on your credit card. Call and ask. Tell them you are tired of paying too much, feel your rate is too high, and feel you should take your business elsewhere.

You can also ask for help. Call utility providers such as your electric utility, and ask for ways you can save money on your utility bills. Most utilities send you free information; some even send a person to your home to find ways to cut your utility bill. Most companies help if you ask; if they won't help you, and you have a choice of service providers, find another company that will.

Step 5: Build a Budget

I know: most people hate budgets. Whenever I talk about budgets, someone always says, "I don't need a budget. Budgets don't work for everybody. After all, millionaires don't live by a budget; they spend what they want, right?"

That's not true at all. Millionaires became millionaires by budgeting and controlling expenses, and they maintain their wealth using the same approach. The largest, most successful companies in the world operate by budgets, incredibly detailed budgets. Budgeting helps successful companies maintain their position in the marketplace.

Budgeting and controlling expenses are two keys to building wealth. Even so, if you hate the idea of creating a budget, don't worry: you already have. Once you worked through every item on the worksheet, your new amount figures automatically create your monthly budget. Once you have eliminated what you don't need to spend and have reduced what you spend on the items you need to spend money on, you know exactly what you will spend each month.

The beauty of this approach is you significantly reduced your spending while creating a budget you truly understand at a micro level. You know exactly where you started and exactly where you are today.

Just for fun—and it will be fun—take a second and look at your reduce spending worksheet. Add up the "Current Amount" column and then the "New Amount" column, and subtract. The difference is how much you've saved. If you haven't put hundreds of dollars back in your pocket, go back and try again. There's more "gold" to be mined on your worksheet. I promise.

In fact, schedule a date—one month, three months, six months, whatever you think makes sense—to go back and revisit the worksheet to see if you can find additional ways to cut expenses. Your situation will change over time. The best plans change with the times.

Bottom line. You can make all the money in the world, but if you spend all the money in the world, plus a dollar, you end up with a negative net worth.

Now that you understand your spending, take the steps to create a method to ensure you stay within your budget.

Step 6: Stay on Track

Tracking your budget progress isn't hard. A wide variety of tools and methods are available, both offline and online, to help you. The key is to find a method that works for you. Remember, you don't work for your system; your system works for and serves you. If it doesn't, use a different system.

Let's look at two very different systems you can adopt. One is basic, the other relatively high-tech. Neither is better or worse than the other; each is just different. The best system is the one that works best for you.

The Envelope System

The envelope method of budgeting instantly structures your everyday spending. Here's how to set it up:

- Use the result of the reduce spending exercise to determine the weekly amounts you spend in your discretionary categories. These categories are typically things like food, meals eaten out, entertainment, gas, clothing—the things you normally use credit cards, checks, or cash to purchase. Don't put items such electricity or car insurance or bills like that on the list.

- Grab some envelopes and write the name of one category on each individual envelope. For example, you have a "groceries" envelope and an "entertainment" envelope.

- Put the amount of cash from your reduce spending sheet into each envelope at the start of every week. For example, if you allotted $50 for clothes, put $50 in the "clothes" envelope.

- Spend only what is in each envelope. That's all you get. When you've spent it all, you're done for the week. Period. No exceptions.

- If you have cash left over at the end of the week, don't spend it somewhere else or use it the following week. Put that money toward a debt you're paying off and later toward your investments. For example, if you still have $30 left over in your "entertainment" envelope, add that $30 to your next credit card payment.

You're probably thinking, "But wait a minute; that's really inconvenient. What if I need my clothing money and the envelope is at home?"

Inconvenience breeds savings: you'll have to think twice about the purchase.

Another beauty of the envelope system is that it helps you keep track of your spending and your goals. When you use a debit card or credit card, making purchases is easy, and the amount you spend adds up quickly, without your knowing it, until the bill arrives, of course. As I mentioned earlier, the average person spends 17 percent to 21 percent more on discretionary items when using plastic instead of cash, and that money could have gone to paying down debt or could have been invested for retirement. With the envelope system, you always know exactly where you stand.

The envelope system works for many people. One person I know used the envelope system to stay on top of his finances while he worked his way through college. Six months after he graduated, he used the money he saved to make a down payment on his first house.

Online Tracking Systems

At the opposite end of the technology spectrum are online budget-tracking systems, like Mint.com and Mvelopes.com. There are also phone apps like Adaptu. A number of these services are free and low-cost. We'll use the service at Mint.com as an example, and here's how it works:

- **Determine where your money goes**. Luckily you've already pulled together all the information you need by working through your reduce-spending worksheet. Enter this data on the forms on Mint.com, and the system tells you the following:
  - Your average monthly spending across all your bank and credit accounts
  - Your major categories of spending: utilities, household, loans, shopping, etc.
  - Which categories you spend the most money on and how that compares to others in your financial situation

Mint also helps you categorize and classify debit or credit card transactions. And it updates your accounts automatically. You can get a real-time, up-to-the-minute picture of your spending and your budget.

- **Set achievable targets for future spending**. Which, of course, you've already done as well, but Mint makes it easy for you to update your categories and spending amounts, especially when you begin to pay off debt. Then, once you've used the service for a few months, you'll have built a history that gives you an overview of your spending habits. You'll be able to instantly see where you've done well and where you've struggled to stick with your plan.

- **See real-time data**. Once you start tracking expenses and identifying weaknesses, you can stay on top of your spending. You don't have to wait for bank statements or credit card statements. You'll know where you stand in minutes. (The envelope system does this for you too.)
- **Analyze your spending and get advice**. Mint will analyze your spending patterns and recommend choices or opportunities you might not be aware of. Some will be offers from other credit card companies or financial service providers, but that's OK. You don't have to switch cards or purchase any other services unless you decide that's in your best interest.

Decide which is the best system for you. If you like online tools, travel a lot, or simply like the idea of an online budget tracking system, give a service such as Mint a try. If that seems more complicated than it's worth, or you don't always have access to the Internet, stick to a simple system such as the Envelope system. Or just grab a pad of paper and a pencil.

Bottom line. You don't need fancy software or systems. You can maintain and track your budget—really, your entire financial life—on paper. What you *do* need is the motivation to stick to your plan and commit to achieving financial freedom. So try a system, see how it works for you, and if it's not working, try something else. But no matter what you do, act.

You can apply the same principles to any purchase. Some years ago I bought my wife a ski boat for her birthday. I looked for a used ski boat for about a year; boats are very expensive, and, unfortunately, even used boats are expensive because people tend to buy them with no money down. As a result they owe more than the boat is worth within six months. The boat depreciates quickly and the loan balance doesn't go down nearly as fast. But I was patient. I knew I would get a great deal eventually.

An old saying goes like this: "The two happiest days of a boat owner's life is the day he buys the boat and the day he sells it." I found a doctor about 700 miles away selling a six-month-old, top-of-the-line ski boat for $19,000. At the time it cost $30,000 new. He was offering a good deal, but I wanted to do better, so I negotiated the price down to $15,000. We enjoyed the boat for five years and then sold it for $15,000.

That is called *buying right.* Another benefit of buying right is the cost of insurance, registration, and sales tax is automatically lower too. Put in time, be patient, and buy right.

Now let's go one step further. Let's take the most basic step in managing your debt: cut up your credit cards.

Credit Cards Are Hazardous to Your Health

A lot of people love Vegas. Think about the Vegas skyline: impressive, isn't it? But Vegas wasn't built on winners. And credit card companies weren't built on people paying off their balances in full each month. Easy credit is destroying the middle class. Let's get you off credit cards so the money you spend on interest can stay in your pocket. We'll go step by step.

Step 1: Move Balances to Card with Lowest Rates

If you own only one credit card, this step does not apply to you. If, like most people, you have two or more cards, the chances are each card charges a different interest rate. Also, the rate you received when you first got the card may no longer be the rate you currently receive. Most credit card companies reserve the right to increase your interest rate if, say, you make a late payment or exceed your credit limit. Make sure you know the rate you are currently paying. It might be a lot higher than you think.

Once you know the rate, take the following steps:

- **Move your balances to the card with the lowest rate.** The card that charges the lowest rate is the card you should carry a balance on. The goal is to transfer balances from your higher-interest-rate cards onto just one card, the one charging the lowest rate. For example, say you have about $2,000 on each of your credit cards and the interest rates vary from 12 percent to a high of 23 percent. If you can shift all your balances to the 12 percent card, you'll save a lot of money on interest, and you can use the money you save to pay off your debt quicker. Before you transfer balances, though, see if you will be charged a transfer fee or if you will be charged a higher interest rate for balance transfers. If either is the case, ask for those fees or rate increases to be waived.

- **Get a new card with an attractive balance transfer offer.** If the company of your old card won't waive rates or fees, go to a different company. Some credit cards offer six or twelve or eighteen months of free or reduced interest. Others offer a low fixed rate for balance transfers. New purchases may be charged at a higher rate, though. Again, your goal is to shift your balances onto a card that charges the lowest possible interest rate.

- **Read the fine print.** Take a close look at the terms and conditions. Watch for loopholes or unusual terms that could come back to bite you. For example, the interest rate might be even higher than the rate you currently pay once the introductory period ends. If so, you may want to get a new card at that time, and that could cause a different problem.
  - In some cases, if you transfer the balance from a card within twelve months of getting the card, the credit card company can charge a higher interest rate and retroactively apply it to all of your outstanding balances. If that happens, you might have

to pay hundreds of dollars for the privilege of transferring your balance from one card to another.

○ Make sure you understand the details of the offer and what makes the best sense for you over the long term. Don't dig a hole just to slice an extra percent off your interest rate. Make sure any terms you accept are terms you will be happy to live with.

- **Slice up your old cards.** To have a realistic shot at eliminating your debt, you have to cut up your old high-interest credit cards. Don't tempt yourself by keeping them around in case of an emergency. Don't cancel the account, though, or your credit score will take a hit. Credit scores are based on a number of factors, including the amount of credit available. If you cancel the account, your available credit ratio goes down, and so does your credit score. So cut up the card, but keep the account. That way you get rid of the temptation and ensure you don't dig another debt hole.

Step 2: Get a Lower Interest Rate on the Remaining Card

Now that you have only one credit card, take a further step and get the lowest rate possible on that remaining card. A credit card company will be more likely to offer you a lower rate if you carry a substantial balance on that card, and now you do because you've consolidated your credit card debt the smart way.

Here's how to do it:

- **Call customer service.** If you can, ask for the cancellation department. Sometimes reps in that department are given more latitude to change the terms of your card because they serve as the last resort for keeping you as a customer.
- **Ask.** Here's an example of what you might say: "Hi. I've been a customer for several years, but I'm concerned about my interest rate. I have received offers for credit cards that charge a lower rate. I want to stay with you,

but I also don't want to pay too much. Could you lower the rate on my card by 3 percent?" That's just one percentage you can use; if you currently pay 23 percent, for example, asking for a 4 percent to 5 percent reduction is in no way out of line. Or, if you like to negotiate and don't want to make the first offer, say, "I would like to stay with you. What kind of reduction can you offer me?" You may get a better offer than what you planned to ask for.

- **Think before you act.** Normally, the person you speak with checks to see if you qualify for a lower rate during the call. As a result, you will probably get an offer while you are on the phone. If you like the offer, accept it. If you don't like the offer, ask to speak to a supervisor or a person who has more authority if you still aren't happy.
- **Take the best offer before you hang up.** If you are offered a 2 percent reduction but were hoping for more, don't turn it down. Instead, say, "Well, 2 percent is not what I was hoping for, but if that is the best you can do right now, I will take it." A 2 percent reduction is better than no reduction at all, and you can always call a week later and try again.

Don't feel uncomfortable about calling to ask for a better rate. Competition between credit card issuers is incredibly fierce. That's why you receive all that junk mail from credit card companies. Most would rather cut your rate than lose you as a customer. After all, something is better than nothing.

Once you have a card with the lowest rate possible, don't take on additional debt. Don't *increase* your outstanding balance—*decrease* it. But don't stop there. Work to eliminate all your debt, except your house payment.

Step 3: Use Debt Stacking

To help you eliminate your debt, we'll use a simple but powerful strategy many people like to call *debt stacking*. Debt stacking is just one way to refer to this widely used method of paying off debt in stages. Some people call this technique a *debt snowball*; others use different names. What is important is not the name but the application of the strategy. No matter what you call it, the concept of debt stacking is a simple, easy-to-follow technique to reduce your debt quickly using the dollars you already put toward making payments.

Here's how to use debt stacking: when one debt is paid off, just take the money from that payment and apply it to the next debt on the priority list you create. Sound complicated? It isn't. Here is a step-by-step look at debt stacking in action.

Step 1: List your debts. This step is easy because everything you need is already at your fingertips. Pull out the budget you created and list all your debts: credit cards, auto loans, installment loans, any debt you currently make payments on. You don't have to list expenses like utility bills or food bills. They are not debts; they are payments you make for services or commodities.

Your sheet will look something like this. We'll pretend these are Mary's debts.

Priority	Debt	Payment Amount	Balance	Interest Rate
_____	Store card	$20	$350	20%
_____	Credit card	$30	$800	23%
_____	Credit card	$75	$2,500	18%
_____	Car loan	$200	$8,500	9%
_____	Car loan	$300	$14,000	6%
_____	Mortgage	$1,280	$200,000	5%
	Total	$1,905	$226,150	

Mary has a lot of debt, but it's not as bad as it might first seem; if you ignore her house payment, she owes $26,150, and she spends $625 a month to service that debt.

Notice that we left the Priority column blank for now; I will show you what to do with that column later.

Also, note that we listed Mary's debt from the smallest balance to the largest. Her store card is listed first because it has a balance of $350, and her mortgage is listed last because her balance is $200,000.

Step 2: Make a commitment to pay at least the minimum payments. If you cannot afford to make the minimum payments on your debts, you have a major problem on your hands. You must balance your budget so you can pay your debts on time. Go back to the previous stages and cut your expenses, sell unnecessary assets, find cash, do whatever it takes to ensure you can make at least the minimum payment on all your debts.

No excuses. Do it now. Your financial life and your future depend on it.

Step 3: Put your debt in priority order. Here's where we build in some flexibility. There are two basic approaches to debt repayment:

- **Pay off the highest interest rate debts first.**
  - **Positives:** Higher interest rates means paying more interest. If one card charges 20 percent interest and the other charges 15 percent, it makes sense to pay off the higher rate card first because over the long run, you reduce your total interest costs more quickly.
  - **Negative:** If the higher-interest-rate card has a high balance, paying it off may feel like it takes forever, and you may struggle to stay motivated.
- **Pay off the lowest balance debt first.**
  - **Positives:** You eliminate individual debts more quickly and get fewer bills in the mail. Dealing with fewer bills feels great and helps you stay on track.
  - **Negative:** You pay more in overall interest charges if you pay off a low interest rate card first.

Decide which approach appeals to you. If you can stay motivated and like to make decisions on the basis of logic and facts, prioritize your list so you pay off higher-interest-rate debts first. If you need positive feedback and love the idea of wiping out debts, no matter how small, then prioritize your list so you pay off debts with the lowest balance first.

Bottom line. No matter which approach you take, you really can't go wrong. Both approaches work well. The method you should choose is the method you can most easily commit yourself to using.

Once you have chosen your approach, number your debts in priority order. Here's Mary's worksheet. She chose to pay off the debts with the smallest balance first

Priority	Debt	Payment	Balance	Interest Rate
1	Store card	$20	$350	16%
2	Credit card	$30	$800	23%
3	Credit card	$75	$2,500	18%
4	Car loan	$200	$8,500	9%
5	Car loan	$300	$14,000	6%
6	Mortgage	$1,280	$200,000	5%
	Total	$1,905	$226,150	

Step 4: Use the power of debt stacking. Mary did a great job reducing her expenses, and each month she has $70 more to use to eliminate debt. Although $70 may not seem like a lot, later you will see how debt stacking can leverage her payments to eliminate her debt.

Here's what Mary does. Instead of making only the minimum payment on her first priority debt, the store card, she adds the additional $70 she has available to that payment. As a result, she makes a total payment of $90 per month on the store card, even though the minimum payment is only $20. She also makes the minimum payments on all her other debts.

Some creditors and lenders automatically apply any extra dollars onto your next payment instead of reducing your principal balance. Most payment forms let you write in the amount of your payment that goes toward paying off your balance. If not, contact your lenders to tell them what you plan to do. Make sure any extra dollars you send go immediately to reducing your principal balance. The sooner you reduce your balance, the quicker you reduce the amount of interest you pay, and the sooner you pay off the debt.

So here is Mary's sheet, factoring in the extra dollars applied to the store card payment:

Priority	Debt	Payment	Balance	Interest Rate
1	Store card	$90 ($20 + $70)	$350	16%
2	Credit card	$30	$800	23%
3	Credit card	$75	$2,500	18%
4	Car loan	$200	$8,500	9%
5	Car loan	$300	$14,000	6%
6	Mortgage	$1,280	$200,000	5%
	Total	$1,975	$226,150	

Without making the math complicated, let's assume Mary pays off the store card in four months. She has just crossed one debt off her list forever. Now Mary focuses on paying off the credit card with the next highest balance, the card with a $30 minimum payment. She can add not $70 but $90 to that payment because the $20 minimum payment she owed on the store card has been eliminated.

Here is what her worksheet looks like now. Note the balances on some of her other debts have decreased because of payments she has made over the last four months, but her total payment amount does not change.

Priority	Debt	Payment	Balance	Interest Rate
1	Credit card	$120 ($30 + $90)	$700	23%
2	Credit card	$75	$2,400	18%
3	Car loan	$200	$7,900	9%

4	Car loan	$300	$13,500	6%
5	Mortgage	$1,280	$200,000	5%
	Total	$1,975	$224,500	

Now let's say it takes Mary seven months to pay off her first credit card. Then she'll take the $120 she no longer needs to put toward the 23 percent credit card and make a payment of $195 on the 18 percent credit card.

Let's take one last look at Mary's sheet:

Priority	Debt	Payment	Balance	Interest Rate
1	Credit card	$195 ($75 + $120)	$2,300	18%
2	Car loan	$200	$7,800	9%
3	Car loan	$300	$12,000	6%
4	Mortgage	$1,280	$200,500	5%
	Total	$1,975	$221,000	

Mary will keep chugging along, applying the power of debt stacking and not taking on more debt until the only debt she has left is her mortgage. Then, if she wants, she can use all the cash she freed up to pay down her mortgage or to build an emergency fund or make investments for her future or a combination of all three.

Now fill out your own sheet. First, list your debts in order, with the smallest balance first and the largest balance last. Then prioritize your debts based on the method you choose. Either pay off the highest-interest-rate debt first or pay off the debts with the lowest balance. If you're undecided, choose to pay off the debts with the lowest balance first.

Priority	Debt	Payment	Balance	Interest Rate
————	————	————	————	————
————	————	————	————	————
————	————	————	————	————
————	————	————	————	————
————	————	————	————	————
————	————	————	————	————
————	————	————	————	————
————	————	————	————	————
————	————	————	————	————
————	————	————	————	————
————	————	————	————	————
————	————	————	————	————
Total		$————	$————	

Next, determine how much extra money you can add to your highest-priority payment. Add that dollar figure to the sheet, make sure any additional dollars go to paying down your balance, and make all of your payments on time every month. Then, once your top priority debt is paid off, add the payment amount from that debt to what was your second-priority, which is now your highest priority debt. Before you know it, your debts quickly disappear.

A Note About Retirement Plans

We'll talk about retirement plans more a little later, but for now let's talk about a sticky issue. If you are already contributing money to a 401(k) plan, should you reduce those contributions while you are working hard to reduce your debt? Here are different opinions on the subject:

- Some experts argue you should stop contributing while you eliminate debt because you free up more money to apply to monthly payments.

- Others feel you should continue to contribute at your current rate because the power of compounding, combined with tax benefits, especially where retirement funds are concerned, is too important to waste.
- Some recommend a compromise where you reduce your contributions to the minimum amount your employer will match, if your employer offers a match.

To find the right approach for your situation, take the time to decide what you feel most strongly about.

- If you are incredibly motivated to pay off your debts, reduce your 401(k) contributions to zero. Once you pay off debt, you have freed up a lot of cash you can put toward retirement.
- If you're concerned about retirement and want to make sure your 401(k) account continues to grow, continue to contribute at the same rate, but work hard to cut your expense and free up additional cash to pay off your debts as soon as possible.
- If you are unsure, reduce your 401(k) contributions to the minimum amount your employer matches. If your employer matches up to 3 percent of your salary, contribute 3 percent.

There is no right answer to this question; if you're in doubt, talk to a financial professional you trust.

Take-Away Points

1. It's not how much you make a month, it's how much you have left over at the end of the month that matters.
2. If you are willing to be creative, you can find lots of ways to save.
3. When using plastic to purchase goods, people tend to spend an extra 17% -21% on discretionary items that they really don't need.
4. Plastic is convenient but a convenience that can destroy your finances.
5. Walk away. Take the emotion out of your decision by waiting for a day.
6. Call utility and credit card companies and ask for ways to save money.
7. Budgeting and controlling expenses are two keys to building wealth.
8. Your budget works for and serves you.
9. What you do need is the motivation to stick to your plan and commit to achieving financial freedom.
10. Credit cards are hazardous to your health.
11. When one debt is paid off, take the money from that payment and apply it to the next debt on your priority list.

CHAPTER FOUR

Your Emergency Fund

An emergency fund is designed to help you survive in case you face a setback such as a loss of income, disability, or other type of emergency. Hopefully, you'll never have to touch the money in your emergency fund because that money will grow along with your other investments. If you do need to tap your emergency fund, that's OK because you'll have the money to do so, and you won't have to borrow. Borrowing puts you back in debt. Your ultimate goal is to never go into debt again. That's true financial freedom.

Determining How Much You Need

Some experts recommend you save three to six months worth of salary in your emergency fund. Others pick a number, like $1,000 or $2,000. Either approach is fine, but in the end there is no set number that works for everyone. Because everyone's situation is different, let's determine the right number for you.

Let's work through the process of creating an emergency fund, step by step.

Step 1: Review your budget. Look at what you spend each month. The total is the amount you need every month to live exactly as you live *right now*. That's fine, but if you face an emergency such as a loss of job, do you need, or can you even afford, to live like you are living today? No, you can't.

Step 2: Examine your budget line by line. Which expenses can you reduce? If you had to, could you cut your magazine expenses? Of course you could. Could you cut back on eating out, entertainment, clothing, or other luxuries? Of course you could. Go through your budget line by line, and eliminate or reduce anything you absolutely do not need to spend money on. The items remaining should be expenses such as your mortgage payment, utilities, and food; in other words, spending required for you and your family to survive.

Step 3: Add up your critical expenses. The dollar figure you arrive at is what you or your family *needs* to be able to live for a month.

Step 4: Take a step back. Can you live with the number you reached? If it feels too harsh, go back through your list and play around with different scenarios. Maybe you would like to add back cable, for example. That's fine, but keep in mind anything you add back requires you to come up with money to pay for that item. The key is to determine what constitutes an emergency (more on that later). After further review, determine a new monthly total, if necessary.

Step 5: Once you finalize your list, multiply your monthly total by a minimum of three but ideally nine. The resulting figure is what you will need to live on for three months if you face an emergency such as losing your job. But nine months worth of expenses is even better.

Here's an example, using our old friend Mary:

Emergency Fund

Item	Current Expense	Reduced Expense
Mortgage	$1,280	$1,280
Cable	$65	$45
Food	$800	$600
Utilities	$160	$140
Auto insurance	$50	$50
Meals (out)	$80	$0
Home phone	$40	$0
Clothing	$100	$20
Totals	$2,575	$2,135
Months required		3
Total required		$6,405

This list is a brief example of the process. Mary obviously has more expenses. After she adds up all her required expenses, the total is the amount she needs each month to meet expenses she feels she must keep. She cannot eliminate or reduce her mortgage payment, but she can reduce or eliminate certain expenses such as cable, phone, meals, and clothing.

Now that her debt is paid off, she could put the entire $625 a month into her emergency fund. If she does, in a little over six months, she could have enough set aside to meet her three months requirement.

Before we fill in the following worksheet, let's talk briefly about the number of months of expenses you wish to have in your emergency fund. You should shoot to have at least three months' of expenses. Ideally, you should have nine. That way if you lose your job, you won't panic. You can take the time to find another job without worrying about putting food on the table. In tough economic times, jobs are hard to find. The bigger your cushion, the greater your chances of finding the right job instead of the first job you are offered, and the lower your levels of stress.

Now, enter your expenses on the following worksheet. Note the current amount for each item and the amount you will need once you eliminate or reduce spending for that item. Then add up the totals for each column, and multiply the reduced expense total by the number of months' worth of expenses you wish to have in your emergency fund.

Emergency Fund

Item	Current Expense	Reduced Expense
Rent/mortgage	_____	_____
Utilities	_____	_____
Food	_____	_____
_____	_____	_____
_____	_____	_____
_____	_____	_____
_____	_____	_____
_____	_____	_____
_____	_____	_____
_____	_____	_____
_____	_____	_____
_____	_____	_____
_____	_____	_____
_____	_____	_____
Totals	_____	$_____
Months required		3
Total required		$_____

But three months' worth of expenses might not be enough. It bears repeating: my rule of thumb is nine months. It may be sunny in Southern California 340 days a year, but when it rains, it pours. You may never expect to face a stormy financial situation, but inevitably you will. When it hits, you need to be able to ride out the storm. And you'll rest a lot easier when you have a nice cushion.

Where emergency funds are concerned, I like to think of Proverbs 21:20: "In the house of the wise are stores of choice food and oil, but a foolish man devours all he has." God wants us to save for a rainy day. No matter where you live, you must be prepared for stormy weather.

Once you have an emergency fund in place, take the time to decide what constitutes an emergency. *Emergency* means different things to different people. A true emergency is an event that affects your health or your ability to pay your bills. Losing your job, spending time in the hospital, or being disabled, even for a short period, is an emergency. Finding out your favorite store is having a storewide, 20 percent off sale is not an emergency. Clothes, birthday presents, vacations, Christmas presents, and cosmetic surgery are not emergency items.

If you take the time now to decide what you feel constitutes a real emergency, when and if the unexpected does happen, you will know how to respond. For example, if you have two cars and one breaks down, you might consider the repair expense a wise use of your emergency fund. Or you might decide that you and your spouse can share a car or ride with someone else for the week or two it takes you to save enough to have repairs made.

Any money you pull from your emergency must be returned as quickly as possible, so you will have to come up with additional funds at some point anyway. Better yet, leave your emergency fund alone. If nothing else, the list of true emergencies you create can help you avoid uncertainty during stressful times. Avoiding additional stress is always a good idea.

The best place to put your emergency funds is in a regular savings account. You do not want your funds to fluctuate in value. One thousand dollars today is one thousand dollars tomorrow, the last thing you want is to put your emergency fund in the stock market and your $20,000 becomes $10,000 overnight. Now, if your emergency fund is greater than $10,000, I would use the concept of a CD (certificate of deposit) ladder. You divide your emergency fund into four equal amounts. Using the $10,000 for example, you would split it into four equal amounts of $2,500. You then would buy a three month, six month, nine month and one year CD with them. Now every three months when a CD comes due, you would roll it over into a one year CD. This allows you to access part of your money every three months, to capture higher interest rates as they increase, and earn a better interest rate then a good old fashion savings account. And, if you have to break a CD early, the penalty will be less. Keep your emergency funds safely invested.

Take-Away Points

1. **Emergency fund helps you survive a loss of income, disability or other type of disaster without going further in debt..**
2. **Emergency fund should be equal to 6 to 9 months of living expenses.**
3. **Emergency fund should be invested in a stable, secure place like a savings account.**
4. **A CD ladder would be good strategy for savings over $10,000.**

CHAPTER FIVE

Your Principal Residence

Let's talk about home ownership in general. For most people, their home is their largest asset. If you own your own home, work on increasing its value in ways that will pay off when you eventually sell it. Your home is a place to live *and* an investment. Don't wait to perform maintenance or make improvements. Do it now. You'll increase the value of your home and enjoy it more.

Better to Own

Generally, it's better to buy than to rent a home but not always. For the last seven years, renting made more cents (no pun intended) then buying a home. The prices of homes where I live were incredibly overvalued, and it had been cheaper to rent than to buy, even after taking into consideration the tax benefits of home ownership.

When houses are fairly priced, buy your home using a fixed-rate, fifteen-year mortgage at a low interest rate. Never take out a thirty-year or forty-year mortgage; in financial terms, that's nearly the same as renting. Say you purchase a $350,000 home. If you finance the purchase over fifteen years instead of thirty years, you'll save approximately $200,000 in interest expense, and those savings go into *your* pocket. I would rather pay Uncle Sam $3,000 more in taxes than pay a lender $12,000 more in interest each year. Tax write-offs are often but not always handy.

Some of my clients say, "I need to buy a house; my taxes are killing me." But are they really? Look at the true cost of buying a house, including interest expenses, property taxes, repairs, and upkeep, and compare those expenses to the cost of renting. When homes are fairly priced, buying makes sense. When homes are overvalued, no amount of tax benefits outweighs the financial negatives.

Most people tend to buy more house than they can afford, they use an adjustable rate mortgage or a 30 to 40 year mortgage just to keep their payments manageable. There is pressure from the realtor, the loan broker, your spouse or even your mind telling you can afford it. The bottom line is, buy a home that you can comfortably afford, financed with a fifteen year mortgage. As time goes by and you can afford to buy a larger house, why not turn your existing house into a rental property and then buy another house, again financed over fifteen years. Wouldn't it be nice to have two homes free and clear within 20 years: one of them paying you a nice cash flow each month? We will discuss rental properties in another chapter.

Paying Down the Mortgage

Now let's take things a step further and look at paying down—and eventually paying off—your mortgage. You might be surprised we waited until now to focus on paying off your mortgage. After all, one of our goals is debt elimination, right? And almost every family's biggest debt is their mortgage, right? Correct, and correct again.

Think about it this way. Unless you took out a subprime mortgage, the interest rate you pay on your home loan is probably the lowest out of any of your other debts. For that reason alone, it made perfect sense to leave that debt until last.

We focused on building a retirement plan through a 401(k) or IRAs so you can take advantage of the power of compounding. The longer your money is invested, the more it can grow, and the bigger your retirement nest egg will be. The sooner you get started investing for retirement, the more money you'll have, and possibly the sooner you'll be able to retire. It's that simple.

So now that you have paid off short-term debt and you're investing every month for your retirement, it's time to tackle your mortgage. When your mortgage is paid off, imagine how much cash you'll have freed up every month to enjoy financial freedom.

Before we tackle your mortgage, let's take a step back. It's only fair we address the fact that experts disagree on whether to pay off a home mortgage early.

Some experts feel you should never pay off your mortgage early. Their reasoning is that inflation slowly devalues the value of the dollar, and someday you will be making a mortgage payment that will seem low. If you make $20 an hour today and in twenty years you make $30 because of inflation, your $1,000 house payment won't seem nearly so high to you anymore.

Others think you should pay off your mortgage first, even before investing. That way you can be debt free. If an emergency occurs, you'll be safer because your monthly expenses are lower, and you can sell your house and use the proceeds to live on. (There's a depressing thought.)

I recommend combining both schools of thought to create a blended plan. Invest for your future *and* pay down your mortgage. That way you take advantage of the power of compounding and the tax advantages of your 401(k) or your IRAs. At the same time, you reduce your overall debt and increase your net worth.

With that said, let's pay down your mortgage.

The steps are easy. Look at your budget. As you know, the difference in your net pay (the amount you bring home) and your expenses is the money you have left for investing, paying off debt, and other things. If you're contributing to a 401(k), then the math is already done for you; that money has already been deducted from your pay. If you're contributing to an IRA, that amount should be reflected in your monthly expenses. Either way, you know what's left over.

Now, simply apply that amount to your mortgage payment. In effect you're applying the principles of debt stacking to your mortgage by adding your freed-up cash to your minimum payment.

Here's an example of what your mortgage statement receipt might look like:

Minimum Payment	**$2,000**
Late charges	_____
Other fees	_____
Additional principal	_____
Total Payment	_____

Most people make the minimum payment. To pay off your loan early, simply write in the extra amount you are paying, but make sure you put it in the additional principal category; otherwise, your lender may apply it to the interest you owe instead, which increases the length of time it takes you to pay off your loan.

If you can put an extra $200 toward your mortgage each month, the statement you mail in with your payment should look like this:

Minimum payment	**$2,000**
Late charges	_____
Other fees	_____
Additional principal	**$200**
Total payment	**$2,200**

To see how this works, let's use an example. Say you just bought a house and have a $200,000 mortgage at 7 percent interest for thirty years. Your starting monthly payment (excluding any escrow charges) is $1,331. If you always make that payment, it will take you thirty years to pay off the loan, and you will have paid $279,000 in interest.

Now say you can put an extra $200 a month toward your mortgage. The results are staggering:

- You pay off your mortgage nine years and five months early.
- You save $101,017 in total interest.
- Because you have paid off your mortgage early, after a little over twenty years, you live debt free and put $1,531 a month into your savings. That's the amount of your monthly mortgage payment. As a result, each year you'll put over $18,000 into your savings.

See? Financial freedom is easier to reach than you imagined. At this point you're investing for your retirement, reducing your overall debt, and increasing your net worth, and the future looks incredibly bright.

A Note About Retirement

Once you are fully funding your 401(k) or your IRAs, you might consider putting all your remaining funds into paying off your mortgage. That works for some people. The thought of being totally debt free is incredibly exciting and motivating. Paying off their mortgage early is a dream they want to see come true. Other people choose to put some of their additional funds into other investments while still putting some money each month toward paying off their mortgage early. Only you can decide what's right for you.

Sit down with your spouse, or a cup of coffee, and think. If you feel your job prospects are uncertain, you might want to put some of your extra cash into an investment you can tap if you are laid off. You might also feel that way if you have a large family and are worried about college expenses or even just daily expenses.

If you are single and you have no dependents, you might feel comfortable enough from having an emergency fund in place that you're OK with putting all your extra cash into paying off your mortgage early.

Think about your situation, your needs, and your concern about the future. When you do, you'll quickly determine the right balance of mortgage payoff and investment funds. But no matter what balance you arrive at, don't spend the surplus. Make it work for you.

Take-Away Points

1. Your home is a place to live and an investment.
2. Buy your home with a fixed rate, 15 year mortgage.
3. Don't buy more house than you can afford today.
4. Perform maintenance and make improvements as needed, it will help the value of the home and you can enjoy them.
5. Don't spend surplus funds, make it work for you.
6. Simplify your lifestyle to multiply your wealth.

CHAPTER SIX

Retirement Plans

Time is the most precious asset any of us has. Time can be our friend or our enemy. There are only so many minutes, hours, and seconds in a day. When time is gone, it is gone. All of us should be better stewards of this incredibly precious commodity. After all, we can always earn more money, but we can never get more time.

Think of it this way: if you are forty-five years old, and like the average person, you have only 1,820 Sundays remaining. That sure puts things in perspective.

How many times have you sat through a boring movie only to say, "Boy, that was a waste of two hours"? Those two hours are gone, never to return. Time affects our investments, our business, our family, and our friends. Life is all about balance. We must spend this precious commodity on developing income, managing our investments, enjoying our families and friends, and staying healthy. Otherwise, time becomes our enemy.

On the other hand, time can be our friend, especially where investing is concerned. Take the concept of compound interest. Say you invest $20,000 a year for twenty-five years at an 8 percent rate of return ($20,000 × 25 = $500,000). But when you factor in the power of compound interest, after twenty-five years, you will have $1,426,000.

Let's start with a simple but powerful concept. You absolutely must pay yourself first. Wealthy people save first; then they pay others. People who are broke pay everyone else first and do something with whatever is left. The problem is there is never anything left over. There are always wants disguised as necessities. Live a simple life, and you will have money to invest and grow, and one day you may not *have* to work, but you may decide to work because you *want* to. And if you don't want to work, you can retire on your terms. Sadly, nearly half of all Americans have less than $10,000 saved for their retirement. Let's make sure you're not one of them.

Step 1: Max Out Contributions to a 401(k)

If you're an employee and you aren't taking advantage of your company's 401(k) plan, you're crazy. If you're under thirty and you start saving now, you could easily have $1 million to $2 million or more put aside for retirement by the time you're in your sixties. A 401(k) gets you the following:

- A lower taxable income, lowering what you pay in taxes each year
- Automatic savings, and earnings, because the money is automatically taken from your paycheck
- In many cases, free money from your employer
- The opportunity to retire on your terms, at the level of lifestyle you hope to live

Even if you're in your fifties, a 401(k) is a great retirement savings tool. Even though you won't get the full advantage of decades of compound earnings, you enjoy all the other benefits.

Bottom line. There is no reason not to invest in a 401(k) plan if one is available to you. Once you have paid off your debt and your emergency fund is in place, go after your 401(k).

Brief Background Information

Although you could, if you want, simply go to work tomorrow and sign up for your company's plan, you should know more about how 401(k) plans work. That way you'll be sure to take advantage of all the benefits available.

Let's start with the basics. 401(k) plans are considered *defined contribution plans.* Other defined contribution plans include profit-sharing plans and IRAs. They're called defined contribution plans because the amount that is contributed is defined by either the employee (that's you) or the employer.

Four things make a 401(k) plan different from other retirement plans:

1. When you participate in a 401(k) plan, *you* decide how much money you want to contribute. Under normal circumstances you can contribute as much as 15 percent of your gross pay, but your employer does have the right to limit the total amount you contribute. Few, however, impose limits.

2. The money you contribute comes out of your check before you are taxed and before you can spend it. That makes a 401(k) plan the easiest way to save for your retirement. In effect you pay less tax each pay period and each year because your income is "lower."

3. Many employers match a portion of your contribution. The matched amount is in effect free money. It's like your employer's gift to you, as long as you participate in the plan, of course.

4. Your money is held by a third-party investment firm, not by your employer. So your money is safe even if your employer goes out of business. You also get to choose how the money is invested; the investment firm gives you a lot of options.

You're in charge, your taxes are reduced, your employer gives you free money, and your investments are protected even if your company goes out of business. What's not to love about a 401(k)?

Maybe one thing: if you withdraw your money before you reach age fifty-nine and a half, you have to pay taxes on the amount you withdraw plus an additional 10 percent penalty to the IRS.

But that's OK because if you need money, you can always borrow against your 401(k). And you won't face a penalty or tax liability as long as you pay the loan back.

Tax Advantages Rule

A typical question many people ask is why am I better off contributing to a 401(k) plan than just investing in stocks. The reasoning behind the question is easy to understand: if you simply buy stock, you don't get penalized when you sell.

Investing in a 401(k) is a better idea than making your own investments for a number of reasons. Of course, that doesn't mean you shouldn't take advantage of other types of investing. The main advantages to a 401(k) plan are the money is contributed before it is taxed, and your employer may match your contribution, providing you with what is in effect free money. There are other advantages too, but let's talk about the two main ones first.

- **Investing pretax style.** Doing some easy quick math shows you the advantage of pretax saving. For example, say you decide each month to have $100 deducted from your pay and placed in your 401(k). We'll assume that before you started your 401(k), your gross pay was $3,000 and your net pay was $2,160. You paid $840 in taxes because you were in the 28 percent tax bracket.

  Because the $100 for your 401(k) comes out of your pay before your taxes are calculated, you are actually taxed on only $2,900 in gross income. You pay $812 in taxes, so your take home pay is now $2,088; that's only $72 less than before you started your 401(k). Even though you put $100 into your retirement account, it costs you only $72. You save $28 per month while you put $100 away for your retirement.

  Along with reducing taxes on your salary, you won't have to pay any tax on money your account earns until you start withdrawing it years later. At that point you'll probably be in a lower tax bracket, so the tax hit you'll take will be lower.

- **Free dollars.** Although no employer is required by law to do so, many employers match at least a percentage of what you contribute to your 401(k). It's their way of offering an employment benefit and helping you create a retirement plan of your own. Many employers no longer offer company-funded pensions.

    Say your employer offers a 50 percent match on your contributions. (Many offer 100 percent, up to a certain limit.) That means if you contribute $100 per month, for example, your employer contributes $50; each month your account grows by $150, not $100, even though you contribute only $100. That means at the end of the year you'll have at least $1,800 instead of only $1,200. This is free money.

    There are limits, though. Some employers match up to 3 percent or 5 percent or whatever percentage they choose. They are under no obligation or requirement to match any of your contributions.

    If your employer offers a match, you should do everything possible to contribute enough money to get the maximum available. If your employer matches up to 3 percent of your pay, contribute at least enough to get that amount. If you don't have that much money available today, go back and work hard to reduce your expenses and increase your income so you can make that contribution. If you don't take advantage of employer matches, you leave free money on the table.

Try to Max Out Your Contributions

Initially, you may not be able to afford to contribute the maximum allowable into your 401(k). Typically, the cap is 15 percent of your salary, although special conditions sometimes apply. To keep things simple, we'll assume you can contribute only up to 15 percent of your pay.

If that sounds too extreme, play with an online financial calculator that lets you model how much money you'll have in your retirement account based on different savings amounts and time spans. To find a calculator, search for "retirement calculator" or "401(k) calculator."

For example, say you are thirty years old and you plan to retire at sixty-five. You make $40,000 a year, and you plan to contribute 5 percent of your pay. Your employer matches 50 percent of that contribution. Let's say that over the long term you average a 7 percent return on your investment. If you assume you'll never get a raise (just to make this example simple) when you retire, you'll have $430,273 in your account. Pretty good. On the other hand, say you commit to saving 7 percent of your pay under the same terms. When you retire, you'll have $573,691, or over $140,000 more.

Let's go to the extreme. Say you put 15 percent of your pay into a 401(k). Your employer matches only up to 6 percent of your pay, but that's OK. You still receive free money. When you retire, you'll have $1,032,654 in your account. You'll probably have a lot more than that. If your income increases over the years, your contributions automatically increase too.

That's why you should be as aggressive as you can about what you contribute. The money you spend today eating lunch out won't mean anything to you tomorrow, but someday your retirement savings will mean the world to you.

If you can't max out your contributions today, here are some tips:

- When you get a raise, automatically increase your contributions amount. If you get a 3 percent raise, increase your contribution by 3 percent.
- If you pay off a long-term debt, raise your contribution by that amount. Say you have a car payment of $400 a month. You make $40,000 a year. When you pay off the

car, keep driving it and you can afford to put more than 10 percent of your pay into your 401(k) and maintain the same spending levels in every other category. When you factor in taxes, you can probably afford even more than an additional 10 percent increase.

- If you find a way to cut your monthly expenses, allocate that amount toward your 401(k). The reasoning here is the same as earlier; money you don't have to spend is money you can save.

The best thing about a 401(k), other than the tax advantages and the employer match, is that the money is deducted from your pay automatically. It's hard to miss what you don't see, until your 401(k) statement arrives, of course. Do what you can to max out your 401(k).

Step 2: Contribute to Traditional and Roth IRAs

There are two main types of IRAs that most people are eligible to contribute to: the traditional IRA and the Roth IRA. Although similar, each has its set of advantages and disadvantages when compared to the other.

Traditional IRA

A traditional IRA is a tax-deferred retirement investment similar to a 401(k). The difference between the two is that anyone can contribute to an IRA, even if self-employed and, therefore, not offered a 401(k) plan by an employer. On the other hand, a person enrolled in a 401(k) plan can also contribute to an IRA.

Like contributions to a 401(k), contributions to IRAs are made on a pretax basis. You get to lower your current taxes, and your money grows tax free until withdrawn. You can, if you choose, start withdrawing at age fifty-nine and a half, but you must start making withdrawals from your IRA when you reach seventy and a half.

Advantages of a traditional IRA. The tax savings at the time of investment are solid and could even put you into a lower tax bracket. Your income is likely to be lower when you retire, so you will make withdrawals at a lower tax rate. And your money grows in value, tax free, while it's in the IRA.

Disadvantages of a traditional IRA. Once you reach the age limit, you have to start withdrawing funds whether you want to or not, and you will be taxed on those withdrawals. Most people start to make withdrawals at some point, so in practical terms this isn't an issue.

Roth IRA

A Roth IRA is a tax-exempt, not a tax-deferred, retirement investment. Contributions to a Roth IRA are not tax deductible when you make them, but withdrawals during your retirement years are made tax free. You can start withdrawing at age fifty-nine and a half, but if you choose not to, you are not required to make any withdrawals at any age.

Advantages of a Roth IRA. The biggest advantage of a Roth IRA is that withdrawals are tax free on both the principal balance and all your earnings. If your account has grown in value by hundreds of thousands of dollars, you won't pay taxes on those earnings when you withdraw your money.

Disadvantages of a Roth IRA. You may not qualify to contribute to a Roth IRA if your income is too high. Tax laws are constantly changing, so make sure you consult with a tax professional to ensure your strategies work within the current tax environment.

Both types of IRAs are sound choices, and you can't go wrong putting money in either. With that said, here is some general advice that could help you choose how to invest:

- If you can fund a 401(k) plan, you already have the benefit of tax-deferred investing. In that case you may want to fund a Roth IRA before you fund a traditional IRA; then you can build a blend of tax-deferred and tax-exempt investments.
- If you can't fund a 401(k) plan because your employer does not provide a plan, consider putting a percentage

of your money in a traditional IRA and a percentage in a Roth IRA. That way you can build a blend of investments and take advantage of different tax strategies.

- If your employer matches some percentage of your 401(k) contribution, make sure you contribute enough to your 401(k) to max out the match you receive. Say your employer matches 50 percent of the funds you put into your 401(k), up to 5 percent of your pay. If that is the case, make sure you contribute at least 5 percent of your pay to your 401(k). Never leave free money on the table, and employer matches are like free money. The match is like earning a 50 percent return on your money instantly. If you contribute $2,000 year, your employer kicks in an additional $1,000. That's a return you simply cannot ignore. Then, once you are funding your 401(k) up to the amount your employer matches, and you have more money to invest, a smart strategy might be to invest those funds in a Roth IRA. If you are young, you get to take advantage of the power of compounding. Your investment will grow, and you won't pay any taxes on that money when you retire and make withdrawals.

Let's sum up our discussion. You should always consult with a financial or tax professional before making investment decisions, but here are some basic guidelines:

- If your employer offers a 401(k) plan, then max out your contributions, especially up to the point where you qualify for the most employer match possible.
- If your employer does not offer a 401(k) plan, max out a traditional IRA first then a Roth IRA.

To contribute to an IRA, set up a plan with your bank or with a financial services firm. It's easy; simply stop by the bank you currently use, talk to an advisor, and ask for information on their IRAs.

Then call a couple of financial services firms, make an appointment, and ask the same question.

In either case, here's what you want to know:

- Where your money can be invested. Some banks allow you to invest only in a CD; others offer a full range of investments, just like your 401(k) plan.
- If there are any fees. Some banks or brokers charge a fee to open an account or even to deposit money in the account; others do not.
- If you can use direct deposit. Direct deposit is a great way to ensure you always fund your account; just make sure there are no fees associated with the privilege.
- What happens if you want to transfer your account elsewhere? Some will charge a fee for the privilege; most will not. Make sure you know.
- How often you can change how your money is invested. Some funds allow you to change your investment decisions daily; others allow you to change only weekly, monthly, or even less often.

You can also check out online investment firms. You probably won't be able to talk to a representative directly, so talk to local banks and financial services firms first, and then read the information on an online firm's website carefully to make sure you compare apples to apples. But don't be afraid to use an online firm; millions of people do.

Finally, compare your options and choose the one that offers the best combination of fees, services, and options.

Step 3: Plan for a Great Retirement

How much money will you need? Where retirement planning is concerned, that is the first question everyone asks. The answer, of course, depends on your individual situation. In the end, how much you will need depends on your goals and how you want to live when you retire. You can take one of two approaches: estimate your retirement needs based on what you currently spend or apply the rule of 10/10/4, a formula for estimating.

Approach1: Estimating Based on What You Currently Spend

With this approach, you decide how much to save for retirement by answering these questions:

- **What are my plans when I retire?** Do I plan to live as I currently do? Or would I like to quit saving as much and open up my lifestyle? (Many people plan to.)

  On the other hand, you may be so excited by the thought of retiring early that you are willing to live a lower standard of living, which includes reduced housing costs, traveling less, and less spending in general.

There are no right or wrong answers to these questions. The only right answer is *your* answer. But you do need to know what you want before you can decide how to get there.

- **What do I currently make?** Your current income is a good starting place for calculating what you'll need when you retire. The odds are that the more you make today, the more you'll need in retirement because that's the lifestyle you've grown accustomed to, even with all the changes you've already made to your spending.

- **How much can I expect to receive from Social Security?** Will I get a pension when I retire? Fewer and fewer companies offer pensions, but you may have a plan you were vested in from a previous employer. The money you get from Social Security and any pensions reduces the amount you will need to take from your savings each month.

  You can estimate your Social Security benefits by checking the statement you are sent every year by the Social Security Administration. Your employer should also provide yearly projections of your pension benefits.

- **When do I hope to retire?** The younger you are when you retire, the longer you can expect to live during retirement. Retiring at a younger age also means you'll need to save more money to carry you through those retirement years, which means you'll need to have more put away in savings. The longer you wait to retire, the less money you'll need to draw from your savings and the more years you'll have to save up for retirement, but again, your goal is your goal. Decide whether retiring early or retiring with more money is more important to you.

- **How do I plan to invest my retirement funds?** You may not know the answer right now. In the meantime, if you invest aggressively, you can generally expect a higher rate of return on your investments. If you invest in safer, lower-yielding investment vehicles, you will probably earn less over the long term.

- **What are my current savings?** How much you currently have is important, but so is your age. The older you are and the less you have in retirement savings, the more you'll need to save in the future to achieve the standard of living you hope for in retirement. If you already have a lot in savings, you're off to a great start. If you have little to no savings, the road ahead is tougher, so you need to start changing your financial mindset now.

Now let's determine, in rough terms at least, how much you'll need to retire. One simple formula is to take the amount you think you will need to live on, per year, and multiply that number by 25.

- For example, if you want to live on $55,000 per year, multiply $55,000 by 25. You'll need at least $1,375,000 in savings when you retire.

- But, let's say you will receive $16,000 in Social Security benefits. If that is the case, you will need only $39,000 of your own money, so you'll need savings of $975,000.

- And let's say you will receive a pension of $9,000 a year. If that is the case, you will need to draw only $30,000 a year from savings, and you'll need total retirement savings of $750,000.

That's one simple way to estimate retirement needs. For fun, let's work through a different method.

Approach 2: Applying the Rule of 10/10/4

This method works a little differently. The rule of 10/10/4 is based on the premise that you need ten times what you currently make per year in your retirement nest egg. To save that much, you need to save 10 percent of your current annual income. This allows you to withdraw 4 percent of your retirement funds every year to live on.

Put simply, you will need ten times your current pay in savings, and to put that much away, you need to save 10 percent of your salary each year. When you retire, you can draw out 4 percent of your savings to use as retirement income.

So let's do a little math. In this approach you can use either of the 10s to calculate what you need. For example, say you are thirty-five years old and make $60,000 a year. You plan to retire when you're sixty-eight. To make the math simple, we will assume you never get a raise and make $60,000 for the rest of your career. (Hopefully, that won't be the case in real life.) We will also assume you invest your money in a 401(k), and your employer matches 50 percent of your contributions up to 3 percent.

If you save 10 percent of your pay (that's the first 10), when you reach age sixty-seven, you will have over $827,000 in your account if you average a 7 percent annual return. That's about thirteen times your annual pay. From that point of view, you're in good shape, according to the rule, because you have more than ten times your salary in savings. Then, if you withdraw 4 percent of the balance, you can live on a little over $33,000 each year.

Now let's take a different approach. Say you are forty-seven years old. If you save 10 percent of your pay each year, you'll have only $301,000 in your account, about five times your current salary. So the rule of 10/10/4 says you won't have enough put away for retirement.

Either approach works fine. The first approach gives you a more detailed and accurate picture of what you will need. The rule of 10/10/4 is a quick way to roughly estimate your needs and to check where you stand and how much progress you are making toward your savings and retirement goals.

Take the time to calculate your individual needs. If you need more help, a number of calculators and guides are available online. Search for information using terms like "retirement planning" or "retirement calculators."

Now that you've set your retirement saving target, let's decide what to do with all your money so it works as hard as it can for you.

Step 4: Determine Where to Invest Your Retirement Funds

The beauty of 401(k) plans, IRAs, and other investment vehicles is that you get to choose where your money is invested. Everyone has different goals, and your investment choices should reflect your individual goals.

At the same time, investing can get incredibly complicated. You can invest in the stock market, currency, commodities, precious metals like gold and silver, but let's keep it simple. As you learn more about investing and as you get more experience, you may want to explore other, slightly more sophisticated, investment opportunities.

Decide Between 401(k)s and IRAs

Let's start with your 401(k) and your IRA investments. Let's work through some background information. The typical 401(k) plan provides a number of different types of investment, including the following:

- Stock mutual funds
- Bond mutual funds
- Stable value accounts
- Money market accounts
- Combinations of the vehicles listed above

The question is how to make investments to get the best return and still be relatively safe from drastic changes in the market and the economy. In most cases, the investment company that administers your accounts does not provide specific, individualized advice on how to invest. It sticks to providing generic guidelines. Because our discussion of where to invest applies to mutual funds, stocks, and bonds, let's take a closer look in the next chapter. That way we'll kill two financial birds with one well-placed stone.

Take-Away Points

1. **Time can be your friend or your enemy. We should be better stewards of this precious commodity.**
2. **We can always earn more money, but we can never get more time.**
3. **Pay yourself first, then pay others.**
4. **Employers 401K match is in effect free money.**
5. **At least participate and contribute up to the amount of the employer match.**
6. **401K will save taxes today.**
7. **Roth plans are excellent if you are age 45 or younger.**
8. **Rule of 10/10/4.**
9. **Investment choices should match your individual goals.**

CHAPTER SEVEN

Stocks and Bonds

Successful investors are good at finding opportunities. Successful investors buy low, sell high, and keep emotion out of their decisions. Sound easy? Like most things, it sounds easier than it is. Fortunately, you can get help, as we'll discuss later.

Diversification

Diversification is summed up by the adage, "Don't put all your eggs in one basket". When investing, it is important to invest your money among a variety of investments in the hope that if one investment performs poorly and loses money, the other investments will perform well and more than make up for those losses. By spreading your investments among asset categories such as stocks, bonds, cash, real estate, precious metals and other asset categories; one will help minimize the risk of loss and enhance the overall performance of the portfolio under different market conditions.

Just as important as spreading the risk between asset categories, it is also important to diversify within asset categories. If one invests in a narrowly focused mutual fund, or buys stock in only one company they may need to invest in more than one mutual fund or in the stock of additional companies to get the diversification they seek.

Choosing Investments

For now, you need to decide where to invest your money. If you're an inexperienced investor, it might make sense focusing on mutual funds first. That way you can take advantage of the skills and expertise of professionals and seek some diversification. Whether you invest your funds through a 401(k) or as a separate investment, there are a number of choices. Let's look briefly at a few of the major investment categories:

Stock mutual funds are portfolios of company stocks. When you buy a share of stock, you buy a small piece of ownership in the company. A stock mutual fund buys shares of stock in a variety of companies in the hopes of getting a great return on investment in aggregate. A stock mutual fund may own shares of stock in hundreds of different companies. The price of a share of that mutual fund is based on the value of all the stocks owned by the mutual fund. When share price increases in value, the price of the mutual fund increases. Because mutual funds tend to own hundreds of different stocks, no one stock causes the share price to increase or fall dramatically. Think about a stock mutual fund as one way to have a professional make decisions about how to invest your money.

Bond mutual funds are like stock mutual funds, except they invest in corporate or government bonds. A bond is like an IOU. You purchase the bond, and a company or government entity promises to pay you back your investment, with interest. Bond mutual funds focus on purchasing high-yielding bonds. In general, a bond mutual fund is somewhat less risky than a stock mutual fund, but not always.

Stable value accounts and **money market accounts** are typically made up of certificates of deposit (CDs) and U.S. Treasury securities such as treasury bills. Stable value accounts are very secure and offer small and steady growth. You won't get rich overnight, but your money is fairly safe from loss.

To decide what types of investments are right for you, start by determining your goals and deciding how much risk you are willing to accept. Determining your willingness to take on risk, how you view risk and return, is a key factor.

- If you stay conservative and invest in stable value funds, you receive lower returns but face a lot less risk.
- If you purchase a mix of conservative and aggressive investments, you face more risk but, hopefully, receive higher returns.
- If you invest aggressively, you may receive higher returns, but you face a lot more risk. In general, the more you make, the more you have to risk.

Every investment involves some amount of risk. The longer you can stay invested—in other words, the longer until you retire—the more risk you can typically take on if your goal is to achieve higher returns. For example, if you think you will need to start withdrawing money sooner rather than later, your willingness to take on risk should be lower, so you should probably choose investments like bond funds or stable value funds because they tend to be less risky and provide relatively stable returns.

If you have a lot of years of investing ahead of you, say fifteen to twenty or more, then you can, in all likelihood, afford to take a few more risks with your money. The longer your money is invested, the more time you have to recover from losses.

Then think about your general feelings about investing. Risk tends to create stress and anxiety. Stressing over how your investments are performing is not particularly fun. Think about what level of risk you are comfortable with and then make your investments with that in mind. Most plans let you shift your money between funds a number of times each year—in some cases as often as you want—so if you change your mind about how to invest your money, you can change your investment allocations. Investment decisions aren't forever.

Now that you have a basic idea, let's take a closer look at the different investment types available in the typical retirement plan:

- **Stock funds** tend to be the riskiest type of investment, but they also tend to yield the highest earning potential. Major dips notwithstanding, historically the stock market has yielded an average annual return of over 10 percent. Some years the return is less, obviously, and some years a lot more, but over the long term, stock market returns have averaged over 10 percent.

  Not all stock market investments are created equally. Some funds perform better than others. Let's look at the different types.

- **Index funds** mirror the market. Index funds are made up of collections of stocks that match the market. If the market goes up, the fund goes up accordingly; if the market goes down, the fund goes down at a similar rate. Different funds are intended to match different indexes. The S&P (Standard & Poor's) 500 index fund is made up of a combination of all the stocks represented on the S&P 500. Because they automatically provide diversification, index funds have been the safest way to get a steady return on your investment. That assumes, of course, that the future will be similar to the past. And there is no guarantee that will be the case.

  If your retirement plan does not include an index fund, the odds are good that it does include a fund similar to an index fund.

- **Growth funds** buy stocks assumed to have the potential to grow substantially in value. Within the growth fund category, you may find subcategories such as these:

  - Aggressive growth funds, which tend to focus on riskier but potentially higher-return stocks
  - Moderate growth funds, a blend of moderately risky stocks
  - Value funds that concentrate on purchasing relatively stable stocks, often stocks that pay a small

dividend, which adds to the growth of the fund's value

Many plans offer a lot of other subcategories. Your plan should describe the goals and level of risk in each subcategory so you can evaluate those investments based on your willingness to accept risk and your desire for return.

- **Small-, medium-, and large-cap funds** stock funds often described by the size of the companies they invest in. One way to define size is by market capitalization. *Market cap* does not refer to the size of a company (for example, its number of employees or number of locations) but to the stock market value of the company. To calculate market cap, multiply the number of shares outstanding in the company by the price of those shares. The result is the market capitalization value. For example, if a company has a million shares outstanding, and those shares currently sell for $10, the market cap is $10 million. Now, let's break down each segment:
    - Small-cap funds typically invest in companies that have a market value of less than $1 billion. Small-cap funds do sometimes yield high returns but are considered fairly risky investments.
    - Mid-cap funds invest in companies that have values ranging from $1 billion to $8 billion or so. Mid-cap funds tend to be less risky than small-cap funds, but they also tend to produce a lower rate of return over the long term.
    - Large-cap funds invest in companies with market values over $8 billion. Large caps sometimes appear similar to an index fund because a large-cap fund may invest in all the companies in a particular index, like the Dow Jones Industrials. Large-cap funds tend to be less risky, but, at the same time, they tend to provide a lower return on investment.

- **Sector funds** invest in companies in a particular industry such as technology, pharmaceuticals, oil companies, or health care. If you think a particular industry is on the verge of rapid growth, investing in a sector fund could be a way to enjoy a return while diversifying your investment across a number of different companies in that sector.
- **International funds** invest in stocks from countries all around the world. A number of countries are experiencing phenomenal growth. But with that growth comes growing pains and these markets can be quite volatile.
- **Income funds** invest in stocks that pay a regular dividend. Income funds also invest in bonds that pay interest. Many income funds invest in both. The goal of an income fund is to minimize risk while providing a stable, albeit small, return on investment.
- **Value funds** invest in stocks perceived to be undervalued. They usually provide some income in the form of dividends as well as long term growth from capital appreciation when the stocks become popular again. They tend to have more conservative and less volatile investment returns.
- **Life cycle funds** attempt to provide a blend of stocks and other investments designed to match your age and investment goals. The goal is to create a blend of fund types to match your level of risk and desire for return. Different investment funds call their life cycle funds by different names. Each describes the goals of the fund. Here are some examples:
  - Conservative, balanced, growth and aggressive allocation funds. Each fund tries to be what it is called. A conservative fund invests conservatively and minimizes risk.

○ Destination 2020, Destination 2030, Destination 2040 allocation funds. Each destination fund makes investments based on when an individual plans to retire. A Destination 2040 fund is intended for someone planning to retire in 2040.

Take the time to determine whether a particular fund meets your needs. After all, that's the magic of a 401(k) plan. You don't have to choose just one fund. You can spread your money across different funds to match the level of risk you are willing to take on with the rate of return you hope to achieve.

If you're new to investing, your best bet is to start by taking a relatively conservative approach. Over time, you should learn as much as you can about stock investing, bond investing, and other types of investing. With more experience you will develop a solid feel for how you wish to invest your money and for how much risk you are willing to face.

And while you're at it, feel free to get advice from a financial professional. Here is a quick guide to how you might want to allocate your investments, based on your current age. Where investing is concerned, one size *never* fits all. The percentages I show you will change according to current market conditions. So let's look at a possible allocation based upon age:

Age twenty to twenty-nine. Here is a one possibility for how you can allocate your investments:

Index stock fund	40%
Small-cap stock fund	30%
International stock fund	30%

Age thirty to thirty-nine. Here is a one possibility for how you can allocate your investments:

Index stock fund	30%
Small-cap stock fund	15%

Mid-cap stock fund	15%
International stock fund	30%

Age forty to forty-nine. Here is a one possibility for how you can allocate your investments:

Index stock fund	30%
Small-cap stock fund	10%
Mid-cap stock fund	10%
International stock fund	30%
Bond fund	20%

Age fifty to fifty-nine. Here is a one possibility for how you can allocate your investments:

Index stock fund	25%
Small-cap stock fund	5%
Mid-cap stock fund	10%
International stock fund	25%
Bond fund	35%

What I've listed is just one possible allocation breakdown. Use my breakdown as a starting point. Everyone's situation is unique, and you should always consult a professional regarding the suitability of any investment. Always allocate your investments to fit your financial situation, goals, and tolerance for risk.

Other forms of investing. As discussed earlier, if you are fully funding your 401(k) or IRAs, and are putting some of your additional money toward paying off your house, you may have additional funds left over. You should definitely put that money to work too. Fortunately, the same principles apply to other investments that apply to your retirement savings. You can invest in the same type of funds—income funds, mutual funds, index funds, and others—but you have to open an account with a local or online financial services firm.

Getting Professional Help

Becoming a good investor takes time and effort, and you have to stay focused on your investments and changes in the economy and the marketplace that affect those investments. If you're up to the challenge, many classes, books, guides, seminars, and forms of help are available to help you learn more about a wide variety of investment strategies.

Becoming a sophisticated investor doesn't make sense for most people, however. You already have a full-time job and, in all likelihood, you have a side business as well. You probably don't have time to learn the skills for, what is in effect, another career. A financial planner can help guide you on the path to wealth, and in the process you learn a lot along the way.

If you're a new investor, hire a financial planner to help you now. Then, as you gain knowledge and experience, you can take on more and more of your own decisions. That's the best approach for many people. It lets you get off to a great start while you build your skills. You need to start saving and investing today, so waiting until you know more about investing makes no sense.

When you choose a financial planner, you get specific advice for your individual needs and circumstances. A good financial planner should help you make smart investments that build a bright future and provide for your retirement. But you always make the final decisions about how your money is invested. Hire a planner who has the skills and experience and is eager to help you reach your financial goals and dreams. You can always switch, especially if the relationship starts to go poorly. Never stay in a bad situation.

Here are five steps to help you find a planner who is right for you:

Step 1: Get referrals. Ask your friends or relatives. If you struggle to come up with names of people to talk to, check with people where you work or ask professionals you have worked with: real estate agents, loan officers, or lawyers. If that doesn't work, you can look online or in the Yellow Pages. No matter who makes your initial list, your financial planner works for you, so it's up to the planner to make you feel comfortable with his or her skills, experience, and level of professionalism. Many outstanding planners take only new clients who have a minimum income or minimum level of funds available to invest.

Step 2: Check credentials and ask some questions. Look for a planner with a solid educational background and some years of experience. You can check out the certifications and reputation of a particular planner or advisor by contacting groups like the Certified Financial Planner Board of Standards (www.cfp.net) and the Financial Planning Association (www.fpanet.org).

When you check credentials, make sure the planner has received the Certified Financial Planner (CFP) designation, a title granted by the Certified Financial Planner Board of Standards. A planner who has a CFP designation has met minimum standards and has agreed to follow a formal code of ethics.

Step 3: Determine how you will pay your advisor. Typically, advisors are paid in one of three ways: fee only, fee based, and commission based.

Fee-only planners charge a fixed fee, like an hourly or annual fee, or a per-asset fee. They don't work on commission. If you have a lot of assets to invest, a fixed fee or an hourly rate might be your best bet.

Fee-based planners charge a fee and commissions on investments they make on your behalf. Planners who receive a commission can face conflicts of interest because they have an incentive to buy and sell investments on your behalf. They get paid when they make a transaction.

Commission-based planners charge a commission on transactions. Commission-based planners are like real estate agents, in a way. When you sell your house, you pay the agent a commission. When you buy or sell a stock, you pay the planner a commission.

If you settle on a particular planner, ask for a written agreement describing the total compensation and services the planner will provide. Make sure you know what you will get, what fees you will be charged, and how often you will be billed.

Step 4: Interview. If two or more of the planners on your list have made the cut, set up an appointment to ask these questions:

- What types of clients do you like to work with?
- Do you focus on particular types of investments?
- Will other people in your firm work with me?
- Do you try to hit a certain rate of return on investments?

Listen carefully to the answers. The planner should enjoy talking to you. If meeting with you seems like a hassle today, you can bet the planner won't focus on working closely with you in the future.

Step 5: Listen to the questions the planner asks you. If the planner asks only what you earn and what assets you own, that is a red flag. A good planner wants to hear about your personal and family goals as well as how much risk you are willing to face. Planners need to know about *you* in order to help you plan for your financial future.

Take-Away Points

1. **Successful investors keep emotion out of their decisions.**
2. **Diversify between and within asset categories.**
3. **Determine your goals and how much risk you are willing to accept.**
4. **Every investment involves some amount of risk.**
5. **Make sure your investments match your level of risk.**
6. **Investment decisions aren't forever.**
7. **Always allocate your investments to fit your financial situation, goals and tolerance for risk.**
8. **A good financial planner should help you make smart investments that build a bright future and provide for your retirement.**

CHAPTER EIGHT

Real Estate

Another way to build real wealth is through investing in real estate. You can find great opportunities in any market: up, down, or flat.

No matter what the current market trends, somewhere, somehow some people are making money in real estate.

- If prices are rising quickly, you can buy properties that need tender loving care, or cosmetic repairs, and flip them for easy profits. (Flip is a word used to describe the process of buying and then quickly selling a property, hopefully for a substantial profit.)
- If prices are rising quickly, you can take cash out by refinancing your mortgage. Cash out is a term used to describe the process of refinancing and taking equity out of the property in the form of cash. Americans did way too much of this in recent years, but handled intelligently, cash -out refinancing can still be a viable option for freeing up additional investment dollars.
- If interest rates fall, you can refinance your properties at a lower interest rate and reduce your monthly payments so your cash flow improves. Then you can use that money to make other investments.

- If interest rates rise, home prices typically stay flat or, more likely, decrease. When prices decline, you can purchase an undervalued house, assume a mortgage from a distressed homeowner, or find seller-financing deals with rates lower than lenders are currently charging. Then when the market rebounds, you can profit from value appreciation.

- If interest rates rise, new construction typically tapers off because developers are much less likely to build new homes they may not be able to sell. Less new construction means, over time, the supply of homes should decrease. When the market picks up, supply is lower than demand and prices tend to rise. Real estate, like many aspects of the economy, is cyclical.

- If prices fall, you can buy undervalued properties, make repairs and improvements, and flip them when the market starts to heat up. Or you can buy undervalued properties and rent them, generating income and building wealth.

Let's look at some issues you should consider before investing in real estate. Think about your goals, current situation, and skills as you decide what type of investing is right for you.

Consider Why You Want to Invest

If you want to make relatively reliable and consistent extra income, buy a rental property that will generate a positive cash flow. Positive cash flow (which really just means money in your pocket) occurs when expenses are lower than income on a regular basis. Bring in more than you spend, and your cash flow is positive. Then you not only receive additional monthly income you also build wealth as the mortgage on your property is paid off and the property value appreciates.

If you are less focused on additional income, buy a house to flip. Flipping a house certainly can generate a profit, but it does not generate income on a regular basis. You make money only when you sell. You might need three to four months to buy, improve, and sell a property. At the end of that time, you make a nice profit, hopefully. But during those months, you receive no return. Some investors try to balance cash flow and larger gains. Some own a few rental properties for income and flip a house or two every year to increase their capital.

Consider Your Finances

Before investing in anything, including, real estate, look closely at your finances.

Your Current Income

If your current income is relatively low, think about buying a rental property from which you can get positive cash flow and increase your monthly income. If you purchase a home to live in, think about renting a room to another person to bring in a little extra income and get help with utility bills. In a larger sense, find other ways to cut your expenses so you can make the most of the income you do earn.

If your current income is relatively high, think about a real estate investment where you can make a short-term profit or one that enables you to build more wealth. You could still choose to invest in a rental property if that fits your goals and personality. If you have sufficient monthly income to cover your normal bills and expenses, start saving as much as you can so you can build up even more capital to invest.

Your Capital

If you have capital to invest, you can use it to make a down payment and finance any improvements you make to properties you purchase. When you make down payments, you don't have to borrow as much money, and you may qualify for better rates on the loan. If you are short of funds to invest, you can look for a real estate investment that doesn't require as much cash. Check out loans that require little or no money down, and try to find properties where seller financing is available. Then work on building up some capital so you can make larger investments and explore other investing options.

Your Credit Rating

Your credit rating has a huge impact on your ability to get financing for real estate and qualify for low interest rates. If your credit is poor, your financing options may be limited, at least until you improve your credit rating. Even if your credit score is low you can still find ways to invest in real estate, but you will definitely have to be more creative or, worst case, get loans under a lot more expensive terms.

Quick note. Even if you don't plan to invest in real estate, work hard to improve your credit rating. It affects your ability to get auto loans, better terms on insurance, sometimes even jobs.

Your Debt-to-Income Ratio

Your debt-to-income ratio is the amount of debt you have compared to the income you earn, in other words, how much you owe compared to what you bring in. If your debt-to-income ratio is too high, most lenders won't approve your loan. They feel you already owe too much for what you make.

The easiest way to lower your ratio is to pay down or pay off existing debts. You can lower your ratio fairly quickly by selling assets and using the proceeds to pay off an existing debt. Say you own a car and are still making payments, but the car is worth more than you owe. If you sell the car, you eliminate that debt. Then, if you put that money toward another debt, you decrease your debt-to-income ratio even further.

Consider Your Skills

To build wealth through real estate investing, it helps if you have certain skills. Real estate investing can be work, but it can also be enjoyable. If you like what you do, you are usually successful. If you don't like what you do, you tend to be less successful or won't enjoy your work.

Your Financial Skills

If you think it's tough to balance your checkbook, investing in real estate will be challenging. It won't be impossible, but it will be harder. Real estate investors need to understand the basics of personal and mortgage finance and have a general understanding of taxes and accounting. If you have basic accounting skills, you can take care of your own accounting and bookkeeping. You can save money and stay on top of your real estate investing business by being more involved.

If basic accounting scares you, overcome your fears by getting a little education. Read a book. Go to a seminar. Take a class at your local community college. You'll never need to be a full-fledged, certified accountant, but if you have a working knowledge of the business side of real estate investing, you'll definitely benefit.

You can also take basic real estate classes at most community colleges. Some people even sign up for a real estate agent preparatory class. In most states prospective agents must take the prep class before they take their certification exam. Even if you don't plan to be an agent, you'll pick up a lot of information about real estate in general. You don't have to become a real estate agent to take the class. Call a local real estate agent and ask for information about class availability.

If you don't have time to take care of the books or to take classes, turn the task over to the professionals. Many small and affordable bookkeeping and tax-consulting businesses are available to work with you.

Your Practical Skills

1. If you have repair skills, consider buying a poorly maintained property or one that just needs a little rehab love. Doing the work yourself saves money and increases your profits. Some work takes considerable time to complete, though, so make sure you get things done quickly. Saving money by performing repairs yourself is smart, but time is money. Skills without time to perform those skills are

irrelevant. And the longer it takes for you to get a property ready to sell or rent, the longer it takes for you to get a return on your investment. If you are extremely busy, buying distressed houses thinking you will make repairs yourself probably doesn't make sense. Sure, the more work you do yourself, the more money you can make, but not if you don't have any time to do that work. You could buy rental properties and turn over all the day-to-day management chores to a property management firm.

If you and a hammer just don't get along, you can purchase a rental property in reasonable shape or a house you intend to flip. If your purchase needs repairs or improvements, hire a professional or someone you know with the right skills to do the work for you. You'll spend more, but you'll also free up time for other pursuits.

Your Interpersonal Skills

If you like working with people, purchase properties you will hold and rent. You won't have to pay property management fees, and along the way you'll build working relationships with contractors, lenders, your local government officials, and tenants. And you can go a step further and get your real estate license. Then you can sell your properties yourself and work with other buyers and sellers.

If you'd rather avoid interacting with others, being a property owner will only stress you out. You can still invest in rental properties, however, turn over the day-to-day management of rental properties to a property management company instead of handling it yourself. Let real estate agents market and sell the properties you flip. Make repairs and improvements yourself.

Speaking of stress, if you get stressed easily, taking on too much risk might not be in your best interest. At a minimum you should stay away from owning large commercial properties or buying foreclosures. After you gain experience in real estate, you may realize taking on risk is not so stressful, especially when you have the knowledge and capital to deal with problems when they occur.

2. And don't let the stress affect your most important partnership. Real estate investing takes time and money. If your spouse is not supportive, you'll struggle, both financially and emotionally. If you decide to manage your rental properties yourself, you will get weekend and nighttime calls from tenants. Be aware of the so-called ten-property rule: If a couple owns more than ten rental properties, they probably won't make it as a couple. As with anything else in life, make sure you talk about your goals before you start investing in real estate. Marriage is a partnership. Make your partnership a good one.

Consider How You Want to Invest

Once you have a good understanding of your interests, financial situation, and skills, it's time to decide which types of real estate investments are right for you. You can buy a second home, invest in foreclosures, buy properties to rent to others, and flip properties—to name just a few options. Because there are so many options, the key is to decide which are right for you.

- **Study the market.** Whatever you choose to do, start out by checking **real estate listings**, what's on the market. Start getting a sense of your local real estate market, even if you don't plan to invest in the near future. **Check out properties you are interested in,** again, even if you don't plan to buy. Get a sense of what properties are available, of price trends, and of some of the real estate agents in your area. Someday you may want to work with a real estate agent.

Choose your investing strategy. You might decide to specialize in one type of real estate investing. You could focus, for example, on buying single-family residences or multi-tenant apartment buildings and renting them out to generate a positive cash flow.

You could specialize in buying foreclosures or flipping houses. You can start out specializing in one type of real estate investing and, as your skills and money grow, decide to tackle other types of investing. That's what most real estate investors do.

Consider the Financing

Unless you have a ready amount of cash, you will have to look into financing for any real estate investments.

If you credit rating is high, and you have money for a down payment, consider conventional financing from traditional lenders and mortgage brokers. You should qualify for good rates. If your credit rating is poor, find properties with seller financing or a lease-to-own option. Some home sellers provide financing; you won't have to borrow from another lender. Many won't check your credit and may not require much in the way of a down payment. If you buy a seller-financed property, still make sure you work hard to improve your credit. Pay bills on time and pay off your debts.

Pull Together a Down Payment

Changes to the lending market notwithstanding, it is still possible to buy real estate without putting any money down. But even if that is the case, you usually need cash to pay for closing costs. And you need money on hand to make repairs, to cover emergencies, or to meet any unexpected costs.

Mortgage terms for investment properties are more restrictive than for owner-occupied properties. On investment properties, you'll need to put at least 20 percent to 30 percent of the purchase price down. Investment properties are riskier, if only because an owner is much more likely to take care of a property than a renter is. In lending terms, risk means you pay more.

If you have cash or savings you can tap, that's great. If you don't, there are still ways you can generate cash relatively quickly. You can sell some of your assets. You can borrow against your

401(k) plan. You can try to get money from friends or family who want to be your partners.

No matter how you decide to approach pulling together down payment funds, the best thing you can do is start building that investment fund now. Cash solves a host of problems, and having cash helps make complicated transactions go smoothly.

Build a Relationship With a Lender

Unless you have enough money to pay cash, you'll need a lender. Start building a relationship now.

Meet with a loan officer and review your credit. Review your credit with the loan officer and talk about your interest in real estate investing. A loan officer will evaluate your current credit rating and talk about the financing you currently can qualify for, including rates and down payment requirements. You can also learn how to qualify for better rates, a bigger loan, or lower down payment requirements. The best way to learn about your options is to talk to the individual in charge of making decisions.

Meet with a mortgage broker. Mortgage brokers, are like bank loan officers except they can source loans from a variety of lenders. Sometimes a mortgage broker can provide a lending option a loan officer can't.

Talking to loan officers and mortgage brokers will help you understand how to improve your credit, improve your financial position, and give you a feel for what types of real estate investments might be right for you, at least in the early stages of your investing career.

Best of all, you'll have a great start on building business relationships with professionals in the real estate business. When the time comes for you to make an investment, you'll benefit from being a known quantity instead of a stranger.

Bottom line. Make sure the types of real estate investments you get into match your personal and financial skills *and* enable you to become financially free.

Take-Away Points

1. You can find opportunities in any real estate market: up, down or flat.
2. Buy rental property that will generate a positive cash flow.
3. Your credit rating has a huge impact on your ability to get financing.
4. Be creative.
5. Know your strengths. Make sure the types of real estate investments you get into match your personal and financial skills and enable you to become financially free.

CHAPTER NINE

Employment and Income

Are you doing what you love? Are you successful? Do you make plenty of money? If you answered no to these questions, I have one more question: Are you in a comfort zone?

You might be stuck in a dead-end job because you think you have job security, great benefits, and a nice retirement to look forward to. I know many people who went to work at a job they hated and sacrificed their dreams only to be let go from that job. There is no security when you are an employee. There is no security when you work for someone else. Your income zone is directly related to your comfort zone. You need to expand your comfort zone to expand your income zone.

Most people are afraid to go on their own and do what they love for fear of not making enough money. When you step outside the box, you soon discover those fears were all in your mind; with the proper mindset and work ethic, you can become a success. Success is not determined by what you do but rather by how you do it. Do it right, and do it *now*. Surround yourself with the best people, keep learning, and talk to experts so you don't make mistakes. If you make mistakes, learn from them, and don't make the same mistakes again. That's all any of us can do. The key is to have the entrepreneurial spirit, even if you currently work for someone else.

I have always been an entrepreneur at heart. I come from a middle-class background. I used to take a lunch box and later (to my relief) a brown-bag lunch to school every day. At the age of nine, on my way to school, I would take my milk money and buy candy and gum; then between classes I would sell the candy and gum to classmates for a 50 percent to 100 percent profit. (I could purchase and sell only what would fit in my plastic pencil pouch.) For two years I had a nice little business going that gave me the means to buy whatever I needed or wanted, and did it burn a hole in my pocket! My father used to tell me, "son, pleasure delay" but I spent it as fast as I made it. Brown bags aside, I wish I had embraced at that age the importance of saving 10 percent of everything I made, investing it, and never touching the principal. I would be rich beyond my dreams.

That story leads me to a key topic: risk.

In the 1980s a man was offered a job with a start-up technology company in Silicon Valley. The salary was only half of his current pay, but his benefits included stock options. Because he had a decent emergency fund in place, he decided he could take the risk without fear of the future; after all, if the job didn't turn out well, his emergency fund provided a cushion he could fall back on while he looked for another job.

He was not the first person offered the position. Another person had been offered the position, but although he made a large salary, he also lived paycheck to paycheck with a big mortgage, two expensive cars, and two kids in private school. He and his family lived a lavish lifestyle, and they spent every nickel he made. Because he had no savings, he wasn't comfortable with the risk involved, even though the potential returns were huge.

Ten years later the man who took the risk retired a multimillionaire. His ability to take on risk made him a millionaire. The other individual still lives paycheck to paycheck.

Abundance comes to those who manage money well and live well within their means. Start today, buy a smaller house, drive a less-expensive cars, take fewer vacations, eat out less, cut back on luxuries, and build up a sizable emergency fund. Start feeding your golden goose today. We all need to fund one and it's never too late to start. The goal is to grow the biggest, fattest goose possible. Get creative, be disciplined, and the return will be huge. Opportunities won't pass you by. You can seize them.

So let's talk about increasing your income. First a quick primer. There are two types of income: active income and passive income.

- **Active income** is produced when you work for money. You trade your time for money. If you stop working, your income goes away too. You can work for yourself or work for others, but either way you trade your time for money.

- **Passive income** is produced when your money works for you. A bank account that generates interest is an example of passive income; so is creating an information-based product and selling it online. Of course, you put work into generating the product, but once your product is complete and for sale, the resulting income is passive because people can buy your product while you sleep.

Let's focus on increasing your active income first; after all, if you have to work, you should make as much as possible for that work. Then we'll focus on generating passive income by making smart investments that will grow your wealth and set you up for retirement, possibly early retirement.

Vote Yourself a Raise at Your Current Position

Everyone would like to make more money at their job. To earn more money, you need to justify your added worth to your employer. Don't assume anyone will simply give you a raise if you ask nicely. If you want to ask for an increase in pay, be prepared. You have to sell yourself.

First let's look at what you should avoid:

- **Bringing up the subject at the wrong time.** If your boss or employer recently gave you a great evaluation or praised you for your efforts, this is a good time to raise the subject. If you just made a mistake or your supervisor seems to be distracted—or worse, overwhelmed—by other issues or tasks, wait. Either way set up a time to meet. Never bring up a request for a raise out of the blue.

- **Presenting a fuzzy case for yourself.** Always base your justification and reasoning on your value to the organization. Never base a request for a raise on need. Saying you're behind on your bills and need to earn more money may gain you sympathy but is hardly justification for a raise. Highlight what you have accomplished and the reasons why you are an asset to the company. Use as many facts and figures as possible.

- **Asking for what you want.** Saying you deserve a raise is too vague. Ask for what you can prove you deserve. Maybe you want a 10 percent bonus. Maybe you want a 5 percent increase in salary. Maybe you want to work from home one day a week. Maybe you wish to take classes and are seeking tuition reimbursement. Say what you want, and be ready to justify what you want in factual terms.

- **Getting upset.** Although you may want a raise, your request is a business discussion. Stay calm, stay professional, and stay positive.

With those things in mind, let's look at what you *should* do when you ask for a raise:

- **Put your accomplishments in writing.** Always show facts and numbers. If you say you really had a great year, you won't make the same impression as you would by saying you increased productivity in your department by 20 percent over the last six months.

- **List your responsibilities.** Show what you do, but make sure the items on your list have real meaning. If you are the head of the entertainment committee, and your duties are confined to setting up the office Christmas party, leave it off the list.

- **Prove your market value.** Salary.com and the Department of Labor publish salary data online. You shouldn't expect to make the same salary as a person in a similar job in, say, New York City, but you should expect to fall somewhere within the range for your position.

- **Set up a time.** Don't just pop into your supervisor's office without warning and demand a raise. Set up a time when you can meet for twenty or thirty minutes. If your boss wants to know what you wish to talk about, and you're hesitant to broach the subject, just say you want to talk about your development plan and career potential.

- **Get right to it.** Don't hem and haw. One way you could start is by saying, "I would like to discuss my current pay. I feel I've earned a raise. I would like to show you why." Then show your list of accomplishments, your list of responsibilities, and the facts and figures to build your case.

- **Be prepared with other options.** If your boss responds by saying, "I think you have done a great job, but my hands are tied where pay increases are concerned," strike while the iron is hot. Ask about other ways you can be rewarded for your efforts, and offer suggestions of your own. Maybe you can be cross-trained in another department. You could temporarily take on another position, adding more justification to your case.

- **Hold you anger if you are turned down.** Always be professional, and make sure you continue to work hard and excel at your job. Also, keep in mind your supervisor may disagree with your justification for a raise; if that happens, ask what you can do to earn an increase. Walk out on a positive note and with a plan in mind.

Vote Yourself Additional Work and Income

People leave. Departments downsize. Still, somebody has to do the work and keep the trains running on time. Why not make that "someone" you? Ask your supervisor about taking on additional work. If he or she suggests a small task, don't expect to get overtime or extra pay. Doing a few extra things is like an investment in your career and can help you build a case for a raise somewhere down the line.

Let's say you manage a department in a retail store. A manager in another department leaves the company. Immediately ask if you can take over his or her responsibilities in addition to your own. Although you may not double your salary—in fact, I can guarantee you won't—you should be able to ask for a 20 percent or 30 percent raise because you have taken on additional responsibilities and saved the company money on salary.

If you are a teacher, think about teaching summer school, tutoring students, or becoming a coach for one of the school's athletic teams.

If you are paid by the hour, watch for opportunities to work overtime. Talk to your supervisor and supervisors and managers in other departments. If you don't ask, you don't receive.

Grow Your Income and Not Your Standard of Living

Earning more money is great, but it won't help you become financially free if you fail to use that money to pay off debt and build your savings. Your goal should never be to spend every penny you earn. Your goal is to value your hard work, spend the money you earn wisely, and build a better lifestyle for you and your family by saving and investing.

Whenever you get a raise or work overtime put those funds to work by paying down a debt or making additional investments. Don't spend it. Follow that approach, and you will eventually achieve financial freedom. Spend everything you earn and you will forever spin your financial wheels.

Pick Up a Second Job

There are two basic types of, what I consider, second jobs. The traditional second job is when you work part time for someone else. You could be an elementary school teacher and earn extra income by working as a waiter on the weekends. Working at a part-time job probably does not sound appealing. But aside from the extra money you can generate, a second job can be a lot of fun if the job is related to one of your hobbies or interests. Say you love sports. You may enjoy working part time as a coach or referee. Instead of watching, you could participate and get paid for it.

Or you might take a second job so you can gain new skills and prepare yourself for a new career. Or you might take a second job to make a few contacts to help you when you start a business down the road. If you want to learn new skills, you could go to school or you could get a part-time job and get paid while you learn.

Here are some things to consider when looking for the right second job:

- **First decide why.** If your primary motivation is to earn extra money, the job you take is not as important as the income you generate and the hours you work. If you don't care what you do, hunt for the best-paying job you can find that fits your schedule. However, if learning new skills or participating in a field you already enjoy is your primary motivation, then what you do matters more than the pay you receive.
- **Clearly define the schedule you can work.** No matter what, don't let a second job put your primary job at risk.

Your primary job puts food on the table. If you often have to stay late at your primary job, and your second job requires evening work, make sure you leave yourself time. Don't burn yourself out physically. Figure out what you can do, and create a balance between earning additional income and ensuring you can do a great job at your primary job.

- **Get to work finding work.** Part-time help isn't always easy to come by, especially good part-time workers. Check job listings, but don't be afraid to contact employers directly. A local soccer organization may not post help-wanted ads for referees, but it may have lots of openings. If you have a particular skill, stop by a potential employer and state your case. If you're an experienced fly fisherman, for instance, stop by a locally owned hunting and fishing store and say, "I love to fish, and I am looking to make a little extra money. Could you use some part-time help?" A small business owner might be delighted to find someone experienced and mature to help his or her business succeed.

- **Be clear about what you can do.** Set clear expectations about when you can work. Don't make promises you can't keep. If you can work only one day on the weekend, be clear. Clear understandings and expectations set the stage for positive working relationships.

- **Ask to learn more.** After you have been trained to handle your basic expectations, ask to learn more or to take on more responsibilities. Don't limit yourself.

Pick Up Your Own Job

The other type of second job is your own side business. It's still a second job, but now it's your job in *your* business. Many people increase their income by setting up a side business using skills and interests they already possess. According to the Small Business Administration, more than 60 percent of home-based businesses are service businesses; most of the rest are in construction and retail.

Here is some general advice if you're thinking of opening a side business. As a business owner, make decisions based on financial reasons. Never make decisions for tax purposes. Many of my clients tell me they need tax write-offs. They say they need to make purchases for tax purposes in hopes the expense will reduce their taxes. I recommend *never* buying or spending money simply to gain a tax write-off. Spending money on your business should make financial sense. If a tax benefit is associated with a purchase, great! If not, tax write-offs never offset poor financial or business decisions.

Now let's say you're nearing the end of your tax year, and you need a piece of equipment for your business. The equipment is truly a necessity, not a want. The equipment will increase efficiency. Buy it today; don't wait until the next accounting period. A dollar today is worth more than a dollar tomorrow. Say that piece of equipment costs $1,000. The purchase results in tax savings of $300, so your net cost is $700. You can generate income of $5,000 a year from the equipment, so the purchase makes great financial sense.

If you do start a side business, be smart, be frugal, and make good financial decisions. No matter what you do, remember that the income you generate should go to paying off debt or increasing the amount you save. Increase your income, not your lifestyle.

Take-Away Points

1. Your income zone is directly related to your comfort zone.
2. You need to expand your comfort zone to expand your income zone.
3. Success is not determined by what you do but rather by how you do it.
4. Do it right and do it now.
5. Abundance comes to those who manage money well and live well within their means.
6. Increase your income, not your lifestyle.
7. Grow your passive income streams.
8. Value your hard work, spend the money wisely, and build a better lifestyle for you and your family by saving and investing.
9. As a business owner, make all decisions based on sound financial reasons, and if there is a tax benefit, that is a bonus.
10. Tax write-offs never offset poor financial or business decisions.

CHAPTER TEN

Your Family Tree

When I think of the family, I think of two Bible verses in particular.

From Proverbs 13:22: "A good man leaves an inheritance to his children's children." God wants us to make a difference. He wants us to pass on our "golden goose" for generations to use.

From Matthew 6:24: "You cannot serve both God and money." You serve God, but money serves you. Money is a tool to use to create abundance for your family for generations to come.

Thoughts of family naturally lead to thought about what will happen after you're gone. Planning for your death or incapacity is not pleasant, but if you don't create an effective estate plan, you'll create legal problems and confusion along with the sadness your family will feel. In other words, don't make an already horrible situation even worse.

An effective estate plan does a lot more than minimize taxes. A solid estate plan creates financial stability for your spouse, children, or other beneficiaries; helps protects your assets for future generations; and ensures your wishes are carried out after your death.

Estate planning allows you to determine who receives your assets, how those assets are distributed, and who acts on your behalf in case of incapacity or medical emergency. If you pass away without an estate plan in place, inheritance laws and the court decides for you. Who knows better? You or a court?

That's the bad news. The good news is you can build a solid estate plan by using a few basic legal documents:

- Health care power of attorney
- HIPAA power of attorney
- Revocable living trust
- Pourover will
- Durable power of attorney

Let's take a closer look at each document. Always consult with an attorney when you create these documents; the extra expense of hiring a professional will pay off.

Health Care Power of Attorney

A health care power of attorney lets you designate someone else to make health care decisions on your behalf if you cannot make your own health care decisions because you are ill, injured, or incapacitated. Although they are powerful, health care powers of attorney are also flexible. You can amend or even revoke your POA at any time, as many times as you want.

Many people think a living will is the same thing as a health care power of attorney. It's not. A living will generally addresses only situations regarding life-sustaining medical treatment. A health care power of attorney covers a range of health care decisions and situations, not just terminal illnesses, comas, palliative care, and the like.

Because the person you designate is legally permitted to make decisions on your behalf, make sure he or she fully understands your intentions under different circumstances. Pick your designee carefully. Make sure he or she is someone you trust. The person you choose does not have to agree with your intentions, but he or she must be willing to carry them out.

HIPAA Power of Attorney

The Health Insurance Portability and Accountability Act (HIPAA) governs when and how health care providers can share your personal health information. HIPAA regulations protect your privacy and confidentiality.

A health care power of attorney lets someone else make medical decisions on your behalf if you are not able. That person needs information in order to make good decisions. A HIPAA power of attorney gives that person access to information about your condition and your prognosis so he or she can make those decisions.

Your lawyer will include specific language in your HIPAA power of attorney so the person you designated can get the personal health information needed to carry out your intentions.

Revocable Living Trust

Most estate planning attorneys consider a revocable living trust one of the most powerful, most effective, and most flexible estate planning tools you can use. Unlike a will, a trust helps your beneficiaries avoid the cost and time involved in the probate process. Wills naturally create the need for probate.

Here is what a revocable living trust can do for you:

- Eliminate or reduce estate taxes.
- Give you as much control as possible over how your assets are distributed. Say you have children from a previous marriage. With a trust you can determine exactly how your spouse and children are taken care of.
- Avoid the need for a guardian or conservatorship if you are incapacitated.
- Make contesting your estate plan more difficult. In most states a trust can include what is popularly called a *no-contest clause*. A no-contest clause says that if beneficiar-

ies challenge the estate plan, they receive nothing from the estate.

- Protect beneficiaries from creditors. Assets in a trust cannot be taken if your beneficiaries divorce or declare bankruptcy.
- Control the distribution of assets. For example, you may decide a child cannot access all the money in a trust until he or she reaches a certain age.

Here's how a revocable living trust works. You transfer your assets to the trust. You still control those assets, though, because you name yourself the trustee. You can buy and sell assets. You can do anything you want. Placing assets in a living trust is the same as owning those assets.

But when you pass away, the trust owns your assets and can distribute those assets to beneficiaries you have named. The person you selected to administer your trust must follow your instructions. You are the boss before you die, and you are the boss after you die.

Pourover Will

A Pourover will functions as a safety net for your estate. Say you forget to transfer certain assets to your revocable living trust. No problem: when you pass away, your pourover will automatically transfers those assets into the trust. Those assets don't go into probate; they go into your trust. Those assets are then distributed according to the provisions of your trust. If you put a revocable living trust in place but don't create a safety net with a pourover will, your assets might be distributed in one of two ways: assets controlled by your trust are distributed according to your trust, and assets not owned by the trust get distributed based on inheritance laws in your state.

Durable Power of Attorney

A power of attorney gives another person full legal authority to make decisions on your behalf. A health care power of attorney takes care of medical situations, but a durable power of attorney lets you choose someone to act for you in financial, real estate, and business situations.

But you don't have to give up all control. You can limit the authority by allowing the designee to make only specific types of situations under specific circumstances, like setting up a power of attorney that authorizes the designee to sign for you at a home closing. Or you can give the designee sweeping authority to make any financial decisions on your behalf. You get to decide how broad or narrow their powers are. And you can revise or revoke a POA at any time.

If you don't have a power of attorney, there's no need to worry unless you are incapacitated. If you are incapacitated, a court may have to step in and appoint someone to act on your behalf. Obviously, you won't be able to choose that person or give guidance ahead of time on how you wish that person to act.

Quick note. You could use a kit or self-service system to create your estate plan but recommend you don't. Laws change all the time. Tax laws change all the time. Hire a lawyer to help you. Make sure what you plan is what happens.

Insurance

Your estate can be wiped out by disability, death, lawsuits, health care expenses and taxes. It is imperative to be adequately insured but not over-insured. At a minimum, one should have the following insurance coverages; auto, home, health, disability, life and an umbrella policy. There are a variety of issues that are particular to each state, make sure you contact a knowledgeable, licensed agent or broker in your home state to get the proper layer of protection for you and your estate.

Take-Away Points

1. A good man leaves an inheritance to his children's children.
2. Money serves you, it is a tool to create abundance.
3. A solid estate plan creates financial stability for your spouse, children or other beneficiaries.
4. You are the boss before you die, and with a revocable living trust you are still the boss after you die.
5. Pourover will functions as a safety net for your estate.
6. Protect your estate with adequate insurance.
7. Happiness doesn't come from stuff. Happiness comes from within.

Conclusion

When Paul "Bear" Bryant, the legendary Alabama football, coach died, he had a folded piece of paper in his wallet. It read: "*This is the beginning of a new day. God has given me this day to use as I will. I can waste it or use it for good. What I do today is very important because I am exchanging a day of my life for it. When tomorrow comes, this day will be gone forever, leaving something in its place I have traded for it. I want it to be a gain not loss—good, not evil—success, not failure, in order that I shall not forget the price I paid for it.*"

Wade Cook said, "If you will do what most people *won't* do for the next few years, then you can do what most people *can't* do for the rest of your life."

Get out of the box, act, do everything you can to be successful, and in a few years you will be able to reap the rewards. Look around you. No one wants to pay the price. They go to work every day to a dead-end job, come home, and watch TV for six hours a night, never trying to improve themselves. Success takes effort. You can reprogram your mind, but once you do, you must act. Successful people are productive; they aren't just busy.

Action connects your inner world to your outer world. What usually holds back people from acting is fear. As Mark Twain said, "I've had thousands of problems, most of which never happened." Our minds constantly look for reasons why things won't work; after all, its job is to protect us.

I'm guessing what you have been doing isn't working. The only way to get different results is to change what you are doing. Face your fear, ignore your mind, and act.

Over time, if you expand your *comfort* zone, you will expand your *income* zone. If you're comfortable, you'll never climb out of a hole. You'll never change your life. If your energy is negative, you'll always find problems and disappointments because that is where your energy is focused. If your energy is positive, that energy will create abundance because you will naturally focus on solutions, on wisdom, and on happiness.

Remember, happiness doesn't come from stuff. Happiness comes from within.

You may love a new car, but a new car will never love you back.

Best of luck. I know you will find your own financial freedom.

Afterword

Some years ago, Regina Brett of the Cleveland, Ohio, newspaper *The Plain Dealer,* wrote a wonderful column. Her goal was to set down the forty-five lessons life has taught her. I hope you enjoy it as much as I do.

1. Life isn't fair, but it's still good.
2. When in doubt, just take the next small step.
3. Life is too short to waste time hating anyone.
4. Don't take yourself so seriously. No one else does.
5. Pay off your credit cards every month.
6. You don't have to win every argument. Agree to disagree.
7. Cry with someone. It's more healing than crying alone.
8. It's OK to get angry with God. He can take it.
9. Save for retirement starting with your first paycheck.
10. When it comes to chocolate, resistance is futile.
11. Make peace with your past so it won't screw up the present.
12. It's OK to let your children see you cry
13. Don't compare your life to others'. You have no idea what their journey is all about.
14. If a relationship has to be a secret, you shouldn't be in it.
15. Everything can change in the blink of an eye. But don't worry; God never blinks.

16. Take a deep breath. It calms the mind.
17. Get rid of anything that isn't useful, beautiful or joyful.
18. Whatever doesn't kill you really does make you stronger.
19. It's never too late to have a happy childhood. But the second one is up to you and no one else.
20. When it comes to going after what you love in life, don't take no for an answer.
21. Burn the candles, use the nice sheets and wear the fancy lingerie. Don't save it for a special occasion. Today is special.
22. Over-prepare then go with the flow.
23. Be eccentric now. Don't wait for old age to wear purple.
24. The most important sex organ is the brain.
25. No one is in charge of your happiness, except you.
26. Frame every so-called disaster with these words: "In five years, will this matter?"
27. Always choose life.
28. Forgive everyone everything.
29. What other people think of you is none of your business.
30. Time heals almost everything. Give time, time.
31. However good or bad a situation is, it will change.
32. Your job won't take care of you when you are sick. Your friends will. Stay in touch.
33. Believe in miracles.
34. God loves you because of whom God is, not because of anything you did or didn't do.
35. Don't audit life. Show up and make the most of it now.
36. Growing old beats the alternative—dying young.
37. Your children get only one childhood. Make it memorable.
38. All that truly matters in the end is that you loved.
39. Get outside every day. Miracles are waiting everywhere.
40. If we all threw our problems in a pile and saw everyone else's, we'd grab ours back.
41. Envy is a waste of time. You already have all you need.
42. The best is yet to come.

43. No matter how you feel, get up, dress up and show up.
44. Yield.
45. Life isn't tied with a bow, but it's still a gift.

Originally published in *The Plain Dealer* on Sunday, May 28, 2006.

www.ingramcontent.com/pod-product-compliance
Lightning Source LLC
Chambersburg PA
CBHW060616210326
41520CB00010B/1356